the
SACRIFICE
of PRAISE

Sings 4 Worship™

PRESENTS

the

SACRIFICE
of PRAISE

STORIES BEHIND
the GREATEST PRAISE *and* WORSHIP
SONGS *of* ALL TIME

LINDSAY TERRY

foreword by DON MOEN

INTEGRITY®
PUBLISHERS
Nashville

THE SACRIFICE OF PRAISE

Cover Design: The office of Bill Chiaravalle, DeAnna Pierce
Interior Design: Inside Out Design & Typesetting

ISBN 1-59145-014-4

Printed in the United States of America
02 03 04 05 06 RRD 9 8 7 6 5 4 3 2 1

To our three children, Rex, Lance, and Amy.

They have been supportive in this and all projects that their mother and I have undertaken. Each of them has a special appreciation for the contemporary Christian music represented in this volume.

Contents

Contents

Contents

Contents

Contents

Acknowledgments

Words fail me when I try to express my appreciation to the songwriters who gave their stories. I have gone to great lengths to make sure that all of the facts are represented correctly in each story.

Special thanks to my wife, Marilyn, who was very helpful in reading and rereading the stories, giving valuable suggestions in almost every chapter. Thank you for arranging to have a beautiful writing room built for me in our home while I was busy with other projects. Your loving support has helped sustain me through all these years. Thank you for believing in me.

Thanks also to the Integrity "family" for all of their assistance in this project. My gratitude to Michael Coleman, who contacted me about the project before the book publishing division was a reality.

ACKNOWLEDGMENTS

Thanks to Don Moen, who believed in the project enough to write the foreword, in addition to giving me his stories. Thank you, Byron Williamson, for accepting my proposal even before you had a staff in place. Joey Paul, I greatly appreciate your upbeat attitude and valuable suggestions. Thank you for welcoming me to Integrity Publishers' first list of titles and being patient with me when a move from Arizona to Florida hindered my work on the project for several weeks.

Kim Wilkins was always willing to help me in more ways than I have space to mention. Margaret Middleton and Joe Buckley graciously furnished information that helped me to locate several songwriters. Rob Birkhead was always courteous and efficient in working on the project with me.

Foreword

As a songwriter, I know the difference between a song that I have crafted using my musical training and a song that is "born of the Spirit." The songs that are birthed from the Spirit of God are powerful tools that bring God's Word directly to His people. Sometimes God gives a song of healing, provision, or comfort. Other times the melody and lyrics of a song are weapons to overcome the enemy in our lives.

Throughout the centuries, God has entrusted men and women to bring His message to the world through anointed melodies and lyrics. The pages of Scripture are filled with songs of praise to God, from Moses' song of deliverance to the great poetry of the prophets. Even before God gave us His written Word, people would sing psalms, praising God and encouraging one another with stories of God's power and presence among His people. Contemporary praise and worship songs continue in this great tradition by setting God's Word to music, proclaiming His strength and comfort, and, in the process, lifting our hearts into God's very presence.

Reading these inspiring stories behind the songs had a profound effect on me. Some of the songs were written out of a personal tragedy experienced by the songwriter or lyricist. Others arose from their personal devotions or unique experiences. In each case, the songwriters and lyricists acknowledged that their songs were a precious gift inspired by God. I know that you too will be encouraged and strengthened in your faith as you read these stories.

This is not a book only for songwriters. This is a book for anyone who has ever been touched by the right song at the right time. If you have ever been carried through a difficult period of your life by a song, or if the words and music of a song have lifted your spirit to the very presence of God, then you will be blessed and inspired by reading *The Sacrifice of Praise*.

—*Don Moen*

Preface

As a college student, I was fascinated by a course in hymnology. In that class I learned about the great songwriters of yesteryear and the events that gave rise to their classic hymns. Discovering the stories behind these hymns inspired me to investigate the backgrounds of Christian songs that have been written in our day.

During the past four decades, I have interviewed countless contemporary songwriters and lyricists, learning more about their songs and the circumstances that inspired them. It has been gratifying to observe firsthand the enthusiasm and detail with which the authors shared their stories. I have a deep respect for these men and women and their ability to lead us in praise and worship and in sharing the gospel of Jesus Christ. My goal in this book is to let you catch a glimpse of their hearts, as well as to share their stories.

Often our idea of a song's conception is of a talented musician deliberately sitting down with an instrument with the purpose and determination to write a song. Although that has occasionally happened—and very successfully—that kind of predetermined composition is generally far from reality. As you will see in the following stories, some of the most popular songs were written in the humblest of circumstances by people with little or no musical training. Even musically trained songwriters have often discovered that their experience was not a factor, since the songs came from the Holy Spirit, with the songwriters and lyricists exerting little or no effort.

I have been deeply affected by the humility of the songwriters. In the vast majority of the interviews, the writers refused to take any credit for the birth of their songs, adding, "It was like taking dictation. The song was a gift from God." Several songwriters told me, "The song came as quickly as I could put it on paper." Others said, "I had no intentions of writing a song at the time. It came as a wonderful surprise." A few admitted, "I never intended to sing the song other than in my private devotional periods."

Some of the stories are humorous, some are serious, some are incredibly intriguing, but all are true—true stories behind some of the greatest praise and worship songs of all time.

—LINDSAY TERRY, PH.D.

1
We Bring the Sacrifice of Praise

Songwriting on a Texas Freeway

And He hath put a new song in my mouth,
even praise unto our God: many shall see it, and fear,
and shall trust in the Lord.

—PSALM 40:3

Although many dangerous things have been done on the freeways of the Dallas/Fort Worth metroplex, songwriting is generally not one of them. But that's what twenty-eight-year-old Kirk Dearman did one Sunday afternoon. He composed the chorus to "We Bring the Sacrifice of Praise" while driving on a freeway in Grand Prairie, Texas. That may sound reckless, but it was not really as perilous as it might seem. You see, Kirk was writing the melody and lyrics in his very musical head. He could hardly wait to get home to play and sing it for his wife, Deby.

Kirk is a native Texan, born in Beaumont. This talented songwriter's musical training started early—at age six. He studied classical piano for the next eight years and discovered that piano playing came naturally for him. Kirk also became involved in the music ministry of First Baptist Church of Beaumont, where he gave his heart to Christ at age nine.

Kirk saw a measure of songwriting success at age eighteen, when Crescendo Music of Garland, Texas, published his first song, and Gary McSpadden recorded his song "Hallelujah, Maranatha." But it was a number of years before Kirk began to have additional songs published or recorded.

Deby, Kirk's wife and cowriter of twenty-nine years, contributes to his songwriting as a lyricist. A self-described "army brat," Deby lived all over the world with her military family. As a teenager she was interested in music and drama, singing in choirs and participating in skits and plays. At age twelve, Deby realized her need for Christ while watching a televised Billy Graham crusade. The next Sunday she made a public confession of her faith at the Pleasant Grove Missionary Baptist Church in Dallas, Texas.

Kirk joined the staff of Shady Grove Church in Grand Prairie in 1980. It was there that Kirk and Deby experienced some great victories in their young lives. Deby recalls, "Pastor Olin Griffing often taught on the subject of worship—'sitting at Jesus' feet.' We began to move from just being doers to being worshipers. We, for the first time in our lives, were being taught what it means to really worship the Lord."

While serving at Shady Grove Church, Kirk and Deby entered into a period of their lives when songs began to pour into them.

Kirk wrote many of his most popular songs during that time, and the couple began to understand genuine worship and love for their Savior.

One Sunday, their church hosted a guest speaker named Charlotte Baker, and she taught about what it means to bring a sacrifice of praise into the house of the Lord. The Dearmans had never heard of the concept of "bringing a sacrifice of praise."

Kirk recalls, "I said to myself, 'This subject really needs to be in a song.' As we were driving along the freeway, going home from church on Sunday morning, I began to think how I might write such a song. Suddenly I began to hear a tune in my mind, and within five minutes I had the chorus of a song written—in my head. As we arrived home, I said to Deby, 'Hey! I have this neat song,' and I played and sang it for her. We both liked it, but had no idea it would ever amount to much as far as being used by other people."

The following Sunday Kirk taught "We Bring the Sacrifice of Praise" to the congregation, which included a number of students of Christ for the Nations Institute in Dallas. Apparently the students at Kirk's church that morning carried the new song to their school, which regularly made tape recordings of the students' singing and sent them out to people across the world. The next tape of songs that the Institute distributed around the world included the chorus "We Bring the Sacrifice of Praise." Kirk and Deby had no idea that the song had been recorded and distributed; in fact, it took two or three years for news to get back to them that their song was being circulated. Kirk recalls, "We were surprised at the sudden popularity of the chorus. We never dreamed that it would go anywhere."

The first two lines of the chorus of this popular biblical song are taken from Jeremiah 33:11, and the third and fourth lines mention bringing our "sacrifices" of "thanksgiving" and "joy," which are spoken of in Psalm 100.

In 1990, the Dearmans signed a contract for "We Bring the Sacrifice of Praise" to be placed on an album produced by StarSong, a recording company in Nashville. Before the recording was produced, StarSong suggested that verses be written to go with the chorus that had been popular for ten years. Deby complied and wrote two beautiful verses for the song.

In 1993, Kirk and Deby enrolled in a missionary training school operated by Youth with a Mission and later served seven fruitful years in Europe, still writing their songs. The royalties from "We Bring the Sacrifice of Praise" helped to finance their mission work.

The Dearmans have now written between two and three hundred songs, with approximately 75 percent of them being recorded or published. They presently make their home in Mobile, Alabama, and have two grown daughters and several grandchildren. They are involved with programs and seminars at The Cove, near Ashville, North Carolina, a part of the ministry of the Billy Graham Association.

REFLECTION:

Bringing God "a sacrifice of praise" will cost us something, whether a habit, a worry, an addiction, or anything else we have put before God. But if what we are offering to God costs us nothing, it is not worthy to present to Him. He wants our very lives to be a sacrifice of praise to Him.

2
Shout to the Lord

Heavy Burdens Give Way to Song

Say among the nations, "The LORD reigns. . . ."
Let the heavens rejoice, and let the earth be glad;
let the sea roar, and all its fullness."

—PSALM 96:10–11

Australia has given to the world of praise and worship music a woman who is both a foremost worship leader and an immensely talented songwriter. For nearly ten years, Darlene Zschech and her husband, Mark, have been leaders at Hills Christian Life Center in Sydney, Australia. Darlene is currently the worship director, and Mark is the director of the television ministry.

Darlene was born in Brisbane, Queensland, Australia. She says, "I came out of the womb singing. In fact, I can't remember a time in my life when music wasn't a critical part of the atmosphere in which I existed."

When Darlene was fifteen, her father, who had recently recommitted his life to Christ, took her to a youth group called Royal Rangers. She attended for a few weeks, making friends, tying knots, and learning about camping, teamwork, the code of life, and, most importantly, the Giver of life, Jesus Christ. One evening, young Darlene felt "the irresistible invitation to receive Jesus into my life." She recalls, "My longing to be made whole overtook my limited understanding, and I got out of my seat and walked with a couple of others toward the leader, who then led us into the most beautiful prayer I have ever prayed."

Darlene is an accomplished singer with eight years of vocal training, and she has worked on commercials for numerous major companies. Time and space does not allow a listing of her many accomplishments, yet Darlene was not without her dark days. It was during one of those trying times that God gave to her a song that has made its way around the world.

She insists that it was not a big occasion when she wrote "Shout to the Lord." She says, "I really didn't sit down one day and decide to write an incredible song that will touch nations." She has been surprised and humbled by the attention that the song has gotten, because she realizes that it came as a gift from God.

"Shout to the Lord" came during a very dark day in Darlene's life, in 1993, when her burdens seemed unbearable. To Darlene, there seemed to be no way out of the situation, save for the hand of God. As every Christian should do in a time of perplexity and heaviness, she turned to the Word of God, to Psalm 96. While she read that psalm, her mind was completely centered on the heavenly Father.

Darlene then sat down at an old piano that her parents had given her when she was only five. Her hands fell on the keys and she began to improvise. Soon she began singing a song that flowed from her heart and from Psalm 96, the scripture that she had just read. While praising God in the song, she realized that her depression had lifted and that her faith and joy in the Lord had returned.

During the following days, her mind was continually on the song, and she began to realize that God had given her a worship song. She reluctantly mentioned her thought to Geoff Bullock, at that time the music pastor at Hills Christian Life Center, and Russell Fragar. They insisted that she play the song for them. With many apologies, and despite a fit of nervousness, she agreed to do so. She later confessed that her hands were so sweaty and shaky that it was difficult for her to play the piano. Fearful and shy, she asked Bullock and Fragar to turn and face the wall, looking away from her. As she finished the song, they turned around and expressed that the song was magnificent. Darlene was convinced that they were only being polite.

Some time later, Darlene's pastor heard the song and predicted that it would be sung around the world. How accurate his prediction has become! The song quickly made its way to many other nations. "We hadn't even recorded it, and I began to receive letters from people all over the world who had sung the song in their churches," Darlene recalls. It was later put on an album titled *Shout to the Lord*.

The song quickly went to the top of the worship song charts and stayed there for more than thirty weeks. It was nominated for Song of the Year at the twenty-ninth annual Dove Awards.

In this song of worship, Jesus, our Savior and Lord, is addressed personally, after which is an acknowledgment of His position as our "comfort," "shelter," and "tower of refuge and strength." Even the "mountains" and the "seas" are invited to join the praise of His name. The final line is an all-inclusive recognition that "nothing compares" to the eternal promise that we have in Christ.

Darlene continues to be an integral part of the music ministry of Hills Christian Life Center, while writing and recording worship songs. She has many albums to her credit and has performed throughout her native Australia, as well as Great Britain and other European countries. She currently has approximately fifty songs published. Darlene and Mark have three children.

REFLECTION:

When you and I come before the Lord, realizing through His Word that He not only made everything, but that He also has everything under His control, then we too will see that the Lord brings happiness, comfort, and blessings—perhaps not with a song, but with the sweet assurance that He loves us greatly.

3
Open the Eyes of My Heart

Saved at an Amway Meeting

*I pray also that the eyes of your heart may be enlightened
in order that you may know the hope to which he has called you,
the riches of his glorious inheritance in the saints.*

—EPHESIANS 1:18 NIV

I'm gonna get rich!" Those were the words of Paul Baloche as he joined the Amway organization. As it turned out, wealth did not come, but something much more wonderful and lasting did.

Paul grew up in Maple Shade, New Jersey. A devoted Catholic, he was an altar boy and often expressed his desire to become a priest. But in his teen years, Paul began to turn away from his religious upbringing. He became caught up in the rock music scene and played in bands that performed in the clubs of Philadelphia and Atlantic City. Then, when he was eighteen, one weekend changed Paul's life forever.

He participated in a weekend Amway conference where company representatives demonstrated how people could grow their business. Sunday morning was an optional part of the weekend, so Paul decided to attend a nondenominational service, expecting to pick up some additional pointers on how to become successful.

During the service, the men who had spoken in the previous day's meeting shared testimonies about their faith in Christ. Paul remembers how he was impacted by their message. "They told us, 'It's not about money; it's about Jesus.' They told about how their lives had been changed. I was like—wow! I was really affected by it all." When the service ended in an altar call, Paul went forward and asked the Lord to come into his life. About the experience, Paul shares, "He totally changed me. I started going to church and became a part of the music ministry."

Later, Paul moved to California and began to play guitar for singers who were leaning toward worship ministry. During this time, he attended First Evangelical Free Church in Fullerton, California, and Church on the Way in Van Nuys.

Paul had begun to keep a journal, in which he put ideas or prayers that were meaningful to him. He didn't consider himself a songwriter, but he began to put some of the prayers in his journal to music. One of his prayers came from Ephesians 1:18: "I pray also that the eyes of your heart may be enlightened." The essence of his prayer was a petition, asking God to give him understanding by opening the "eyes of his heart."

There were some contributing factors that had a bearing on Paul's thinking. He had led a great number of worship schools with organizations such as Youth with a Mission, Integrity Music, and Maranatha Music. One day, not long before he penned his prayer based on Ephesians 1:18, it occurred to him that the conferences were good and valuable, but he was not teaching in exactly the way he should have been.

Paul thought, "It is all backward to teach the externals, lifting of the hands, kneeling, and even singing—which are all good. But we should teach people that they should respond to the heavenly Father without being taught what to do. Their response to the One who gives us life and breath should be natural."

Paul began to realize that Christians did not need mere teaching, but a revelation of God and a crying out to Him, saying, "God, open the eyes of my heart. Reveal to me how I might taste and see who You really are, so that I might be changed from the inside out. May I respond sincerely, and not in a way that I have been taught. Help me to have a response of gratitude and admiration, and a sense of awe and worship toward Jesus."

While leading worship during a church prayer service, Paul began to sing some of the prayers of his heart, one of which was, "Open the eyes of our hearts, Lord." That prayer soon became a worship song. Paul recorded the song on a project, but he did not feel any different about it than any of the other songs on the CD. He remembers being surprised when he later heard that it was being used at youth rallies and at Promise Keepers meetings.

In addition to Paul's travel schedule and recordings, he has served as the worship leader of Community Christian Fellowship in Lindale, Texas, for twelve years. He and his wife, Rita, author of "I Will Celebrate" and other popular worship songs, have three children.

REFLECTION:

May God grant us the ability to see clearly today—from the eyes of our hearts—that our heavenly Father invites us to worship and fellowship with Him. And may we remember that along with God's invitation to worship comes an expectation that we should be responsible children and obey Him in all things.

4
God Will Make a Way

A Song Written for One Family

I will even make a way in the wilderness,
and rivers in the desert.

—ISAIAH 43:19 KJV

An unspeakable tragedy gave birth to a widely known praise and worship song written by Don Moen, one of the most influential and gifted composers of this generation.

Moen's influence on this genre of Christian music has been notable and extensive for the better part of a quarter century. He came to that role immensely prepared in every way. He would be the first to tell you that his mother launched him into a musical ministry.

Don was born in Duluth, Minnesota, the second oldest of four children. His mother was a church pianist, so it was important to her that the children be involved in church and Sunday school activities, especially the music programs. She also insisted that all of her children start piano lessons in the second grade. Don reports that he, his older brother, and two younger sisters went to their lessons kicking and screaming for six years.

In the third grade, Don began playing the violin, which was to be his major instrument for the coming years. His proficiency on the violin allowed him to win a scholarship to the University of Southern Mississippi. He soon found himself playing in seven orchestras from Memphis to Mobile.

During a series of God-directed events that took Don from Oral Roberts University to a position with Terry Law Ministries and finally to his present ministry with Integrity Incorporated, he began to write and record songs that have ministered to millions of people. One such meaningful song is "God Will Make a Way."

This song was written during a tragedy in Don's family. His wife's sister and her husband, Susan and Craig Phelps, were involved in a car accident during a ski trip they took from their home in Oklahoma to a resort in Colorado. Somewhere in the Texas panhandle, their van was hit by an eighteen-wheeler. As they approached a remote intersection, Craig did not see the truck coming, and the driver of the truck did not see the Phelps's van. The truck hit a rear panel of the van with such force that all four of their children were thrown out. The children had just left their seats, where they had been buckled in, to lie down for a nap on a "bed" positioned in the rear of the van. In the darkness only the crying of their severely injured children made it possible for Craig and Susan to find them—all except one, their nine-year-old son, Jeremy, whom they finally located lying by a nearby fence. He had died upon impact from a broken neck.

Craig, a medical doctor, carefully picked up his son and tried to revive him, but he later recalled feeling as if God said to him, "Jeremy is with Me. You deal with those who are living." They sat for forty-five minutes out in the wilderness, waiting for an ambulance.

Don received word of the tragedy from his mother-in-law, but he hesitated to call Craig, not knowing what to say. Craig was a physician who dealt with life and death on a daily basis, and now his own son was in his arms—dead. Craig knew the Word of God and had been living in faith, believing the Lord for things in his life. Don wrestled with the question, "Why would something like this happen?"

Craig and Susan asked Don to sing at Jeremy's funeral, so he boarded a plane and headed for Oklahoma. As he sat on the plane, wondering what he should say to them, he began to read the Book of Isaiah. His eyes went to chapter 43, verse 19: "I will even make a way in the wilderness, and rivers in the desert." Through that scripture, the Lord gave Don a song for the Phelpses. He wrote it on a legal pad, intending to sing it at the funeral; but Craig and Susan had already planned for Don to sing Henry Smith's "Give Thanks," so he sang their request instead.

After the funeral, Don sat with Craig and Susan, holding them in his arms. He cried with them, and through his tears he said, "The Lord gave me a song for you." He began singing "God Will Make a Way." The song is a reassurance that God will not only stay close to us as a guide and friend, but He will be there during each "new day." Even though our way seems as rugged as a desert or a wilderness, He will "still remain" as our restorer and provider.

Don made a taped copy of the song for Susan. Don said, "I knew that when all of the people had gone, and everything was said and done, there would be days when she would need to hear that God was working in ways that she couldn't see."

God does work in many ways that we do not understand. Jeremy's friends heard that he had become a Christian before the accident. Many of them began to ask how they might know Christ, so that they too could go to heaven when they died. Jeremy's parents became more intense in their walk with the Lord.

Susan Phelps later related how she made a quick decision between the time that she got out of the van and the time they found her son. She knew that she had to choose between becoming bitter and accepting God's plan for their family at that time. Good things happened as a result of making the decision to embrace God's will, no matter what that would mean in their lives. She agreed that God really did make a way for them.

About two years later, Don was called to sing in a small church in Dothan, Alabama. Although he had never intended to sing "God

Will Make a Way" in a public service—he had written it just for that grieving family—somehow he felt impressed of the Lord to share the song with those people. He did so, and the song had a tremendous impact on them.

The following week Don led worship during the Wednesday staff devotional at Integrity Music, and again the Lord laid it upon his heart to sing that song. So he pulled out his legal pad, looked at the lyrics, and sang it for them. It seemed as if almost everyone there needed to hear the words, "He works in ways we cannot see."

Following the devotional period, F. G. Baldwin approached Don and asked, "Have you ever thought of recording that song?" Don quickly replied, "Oh no, I would never record that song. It is much too simple." Baldwin protested, "That song has a tremendous message, and I think it needs to be recorded." After discussing it with some of the staff, they decided to put the song on a project entitled *Eternal God.*

From that album, the song has made its way around the world, blessing and reassuring the hearts of millions of God's children.

REFLECTION:

Our troubles and cares may not reach the magnitude of the tragedy Craig and Susan Phelps suffered, yet there are times in our lives when we need to be assured that we have a God who loves us and who will make a way for us, even when "there seems to be no way."

5

Surely the Presence of the Lord

A Song When I Least Expected It

Serve the Lord with gladness;
come before His presence with singing.

—PSALM 100:2

Lanny Wolfe has had a colorful career as a singer and songwriter. Born in Columbus, Ohio, Lanny was exposed to music at an early age. His mother sang and played guitar at many revivals and special church services. As young children, Lanny and his brother and sister rode the city bus to church, where, at age eleven, he became a Christian.

His music training started early, and he credits two people with helping to nurture his love for music: Ruth Morgan, a junior high teacher who encouraged him greatly, and Lois Newstrand, a pastor's wife who gave him the responsibility of playing the piano for a camp choir. Encouraged by these women, Lanny went on to receive two bachelor's degrees, two master's degrees, and one honorary doctorate in music. He served as dean of the School of Music in three different colleges and founded the National Music Ministry Conference in Jackson, Mississippi.

Many songwriters have revealed that they have occasionally written songs in a spontaneous fashion, but few have had an experience quite like Lanny Wolfe's one day in Columbia, Mississippi. He was there with the Lanny Wolfe Trio to participate in the dedication of a new church auditorium. It was a very formal church gathering, with the mayor and a number of other special officials in attendance.

Lanny recalls, "As I and the other members of the trio were waiting to sing, the Lord suddenly dropped a tune and some lyrics right into my head. What was unusual about this incident was that the music went in a certain progression that I would not ordinarily go to, especially not being at a keyboard. But as I sat there, the Lord gave me the whole chorus." Lanny quickly reached for a scrap of paper on which to jot the words he sensed that God was giving to him.

When it was time for the trio to sing, Lanny stepped to the piano and began singing the chorus. When he finished singing it, he taught it to the audience—and the other members of the trio learned it along with the congregation! In the song Lanny reminded the people gathered there that the Lord was present with them as they were assembled in His name. They could sense God's "mighty power and His grace." As he observed others around him, he sang that he could see the glory of the Lord "on each face," an indication that the "presence of the Lord" had come into their church that day.

Lanny's song "Surely the Presence" has gone around the world. His hastily scribbled notes, now framed, hang in the foyer of that church as a constant reminder to the congregation that they witnessed the birth of a famous song.

Lanny Wolfe has received many honors and awards as a result of his talented songwriting, among which are being named the Society of European Stage Authors and Composer's Gospel Composer of the Year in 1975 and 1976 and winning a Dove Award as the Gospel Music Association's Songwriter of the Year in 1984 for his song "More Than Wonderful," which was also voted Song of the Year. Lanny continues to write songs and musicals that bless the church of God.

REFLECTION:
The Bible reminds us that our Savior gives us the calm assurance of His presence that we long for in our lives. His glory is our satisfaction and our joy as we serve Him with happiness in our hearts.

6
Great Is the Lord

Writing Songs by Candlelight

For the LORD is great and greatly to be praised;
He is also to be feared above all gods.

—1 CHRONICLES 16:25

"M om, I just saw the girl I'm going to marry!" Michael W. Smith announced to his mother on the phone. "Really! Who is she?" Michael's curious mother asked. "I don't know. I'll have to call you back," was his quick response. Smitty, as his friends call him, had been reading a magazine during a visit to a record company in Nashville, Tennessee, when he saw Debbie Davis walk by. According to Michael, it was love at first sight. He quickly learned her name from others in the building and went looking for her. He spotted her coming out of the ladies' room and readily introduced himself.

Michael was already devoted to his music career, but little did he realize that he had just seen the woman who would write songs with him, give birth to their five children, and be a devoted companion and mother. And Debbie had no idea that she would soon marry the man who would later become one of the most recognizable singers and songwriters in the world of praise and worship music and that millions of people around the world would sing the songs they would write together.

Michael was born in a small West Virginia town, while Debbie is a native of Nashville. They both became Christians early in their lives—Michael at age ten and Debbie at age six. Debbie, who enjoys writing stories and poetry, earned a degree from Wheaton College. Michael, after spending one year at Marshall University, heard Nashville calling and made his way to "Music City" at age nineteen, ready to continue his pursuit of a career in music.

Following the chance meeting at the record company, Michael and Debbie began to date a couple of days later. Theirs was a whirlwind relationship. Three and a half weeks after their first date, the radiant couple was engaged; and four months after that, they were married. During the engagement period they wrote their first song together, Debbie the lyrics and Michael the musical setting.

For the past twenty years, the Smiths have continued a music ministry that has extended throughout the United States and abroad—Debbie writing lyrics and Michael composing music, recording, singing in concerts from coast to coast, and writing more songs, many of which have become favorites. All seven members of the Smith family are active in their church.

Debbie recalls that several years ago, she and Michael used to write praise and worship choruses together during the evening hours. Michael seemed to do his best work at night, and sometimes the couple used a candle for light. Before writing a song, they would read the Bible, and God would inspire their hearts with a particular passage of Scripture. Although many of the songs they composed were never heard by others, they greatly enjoyed writing them together. The songs were the expressions of their hearts in response to the treasures they gleaned from God's Word.

During one of these late evening writing sessions, in 1982, God led Michael and Debbie to a particular passage of Scripture that they both thought would be a good song. Debbie wrote a few lines of the lyrics as Michael worked on the music. The words and the musical setting of "Great Is the Lord" came together at the same time. The Smiths were delighted with the song God had given them, and Michael thought it was something that he would like to share with others, especially the people of their church, Belmont Church in Nashville.

Michael often led worship at the church, so during one of the services he taught the song to the congregation. The congregation seemed greatly moved to worship as they sang "Great Is the Lord." The song lists several of the wonderful attributes of our Savior, including "holy and just," "faithful and true," "worthy of glory," and "worthy of praise." This very popular song closes with an admonition to us to "lift up [our] voice" because our Lord is great! Of the experience Michael says, "I remember I was so overwhelmed as I heard that great crowd lifting their voices in praise as they sang our song. The massiveness of the people around me sounded like a large choir. I felt so blessed to be used in that way."

During those days Michael was working on his first album, *The Michael W. Smith Project,* and he decided to include "Great Is the Lord." Since the album's release, the song has gone on to circle the globe again and again. It continues, year after year, to be among the favorite worship songs in churches across America.

REFLECTION:

In this song we are reminded of several attributes of our heavenly Father: He is just and our justifier; He is love and loved us before the foundation of the world; He is faithful and sustains us by His faithfulness; and He is so holy that we can only imagine, but never quite comprehend, the extent of His holiness.

7
Lord, I Lift Your Name on High

A Small Macintosh and a Cyber Bible

Let them praise the name of the LORD:
for His name alone is exalted;
His glory is above the earth and heaven.

—PSALM 148:13

From 1997 to 2002, one of Rick Founds's songs had the distinction of being the number one praise and worship song being sung in America's churches, according to Christian Copyright Licensing International's Top 25 list. Although "Lord, I Lift Your Name on High" is only one of more than three hundred songs that Rick has written, it is by far his most popular.

As a young child in Idaho Falls, Idaho, Rick became fascinated with music, often climbing up on the piano bench to explore the keyboard. By age ten he was writing songs for his Sunday school class, the first of which was "Come to Me." Young Rick loved hymns and the presentations of the church choir. He also developed a love for the guitar and honed his skills by playing along with television commercials.

Rick graduated from college with a degree in media technology. He had wanted to pursue a degree in music but was steered away from that goal by a high school choral teacher who had become discouraged in his own career. Rick did, however, take a number of music courses in college, giving him the background he needed for his future ministry.

Following college, Rick taught visual technology at Saddleback College in Mission Viejo, California, for seven years. He led worship on the weekends and sang in special meetings with his praise team. From that employment he went full-time into the ministry of music at a church in California and continued there for fourteen years. It was while music director at that church that he wrote his now-famous song, "Lord, I Lift Your Name on High."

The song was born out of Rick's typical morning devotions. He had a small Macintosh computer and an electronic Bible, which he would bring up on his monitor and begin reading where he had left off the previous day. Since his office at church was far away from other people, Rick had developed a habit of playing his guitar while reading the Bible on his computer screen.

One day, as Rick was having his daily devotional, the Lord impressed on his heart that His work on our behalf was a cycle of events—Christ came from heaven to earth, gave His life on the cross for us, was buried and three days later rose from the dead, and went back to His heavenly Father, making the cycle and our salvation complete. That, essentially, is the lyric of the song. Rick picked up his guitar and began to sing "Lord, I Lift Your Name on High."

Rick explained, "It is just a simple song, but it is what the Lord dropped into my heart. The whole song came quickly; I didn't struggle with it at all. I did, however, continue to work on the latter part of the song for another four or five days before I felt it was complete. I then sang it for an evening Bible study. They seemed to love the song. At the time I had no idea that it would be so popular—I had simply written another song, much as I had done so many times before."

Rick was thrilled to hear thousands of men sing his song at Promise Keepers rallies. The song has become widely popular and now can be heard in other countries of the world, in many languages. Rick rejoices in letters of how the song has impacted people around the world.

Rick and his wife, Debbie, have three daughters and make their home in California.

REFLECTION:

There are times when we should worship our heavenly Father simply for who He is. There are times when we should worship God because of His holiness. And there are times when we should worship God for all that He has done to bring us to Himself.

8
Holy Ground

Dad Was Happy, and Mom Cried

Take off your sandals,
for the place where you are standing
is holy ground.

—Exodus 3:5

Many songwriters who have become well-known in the world of Christian music started their musical journey in early childhood. Geron Davis, born into a pastor's home in Bogalusa, Louisiana, is one of those people.

Geron was raised around music. His mom played piano and dad played guitar, and they sang together for church services. Even as a young child of four or five, Geron often sang with them. They would stand young Geron on a piano bench behind the pulpit, and he would sing the melody while his mom sang alto and his dad sang tenor and played guitar.

Geron taught himself to play the piano and started making up songs as a small child, simple choruses that he would sing in Sunday school. During those days he often listened to recordings of his favorite singers, such as the Happy Goodman Family, the Rambos, and Lari Goss, and tried to pick out their harmonies on the piano keyboard.

When Geron was nineteen, his dad was pastor of a church in Savannah, Tennessee. The church soon outgrew its current meeting place and began to build a larger sanctuary. When the new church auditorium was about two months from completion, Geron's dad asked, "Son, would you write a song for us to sing during the first service in our new building?" Geron eagerly agreed. A few weeks went by and Geron had not written the song. His dad asked again, "Son, do you have a song for us?" Geron replied, "Not yet, but I'll write one."

In the meantime, Geron was busy traveling from place to place, singing in churches all over the area with a group of young people from church. He was also busy writing songs for the group to sing. But his dad was insistent, desperately wanting Geron to write the song for the new building. Recalls Geron, "He kept bugging me. I was like, 'Dad, just chill out. I'll write a song.' "

Soon it was Saturday night, the night before the first service in the new building, and Geron still had not written a song. He had worked all day at the church, getting the building ready and putting last-minute touches on everything. After all of the church members had gone and only Geron and his parents were left, they began to check all of the Sunday school rooms and the offices, making sure that those areas were ready for the big day. Geron's dad turned to him and asked again, "Do you have a song for us?" Geron grinned and replied, in true Southern fashion, "No sir, but I'm fixin' to."

He went into the new sanctuary, dimmed the lights, and sat down at the new grand piano. He began to think, *What do we want to say when we come into this building tomorrow for our first worship service?* He began to hum and softly sing some lyrics that had started coming to him. As he began to write the lyrics down, they kept coming, as quickly as he could write. Within fifteen minutes Geron had finished the entire song. He then went home and to bed. Someone asked him later, "Did you realize that you had written something powerful?" Geron replied, "Are you kidding? I was nineteen years old, it was midnight, and I wanted to get to bed. I was too young to recognize the greatness of what God had done. I was just happy the song was finished."

As the oldest child, Geron knew that he could be a little bossy with his younger siblings, so he got two of them up early the next morning and taught them all of the parts to his new song. He had only the lyrics written down, so he taught his brother and sister their parts by rote. The three of them sang it later that morning in the church service.

One has to be amazed when thinking of the theological depth of the lyrics, especially coming from a teenager. Surely Geron thought about the crowds who would bring their needs into "His presence" the following morning. Even as a teenager, Geron knew that Christ "has the answer" to all of our problems and that the congregation could reach out to Him. They had all spent so much time and effort in giving, working, and preparing for the new sanctuary, where the Word of God would be preached, that Geron knew it was a place where the Spirit of the Lord would work in the hearts of those who were in need—a hallowed place, "holy ground."

Geron recalls, "My dad was happy because I had written a song for us to sing. My mom cried because she thought her kids never sounded better. The congregation responded unbelievably to 'Holy Ground.' I said to myself, 'Well, it's a highly emotional day.' It was our first Sunday in the new building, and we appreciated what had happened, but we had no idea what would really happen to the song over the coming years. Even so, the events of the morning made for a memorable birth for my song."

As Geron and his brother and sister continued to sing "Holy Ground," it grew in popularity, even to the point that it was used during the funeral of President Clinton's mother. Barbara Streisand, who was in attendance at the funeral, was so taken by the song that she recorded it and put it on her next CD. It has been recorded by hundreds, if not thousands, of singing groups and shows no signs of slowing down as it becomes one of the most popular and well-known Christian songs in the world. To date, Geron has written more than two hundred published songs.

REFLECTION:

The goal for which we should all strive is to live in such a way as to recognize that the place where we often stand is holy ground, the place where God can meet with us and teach us His ways. We should live each day in the awareness that, with the presence of the Holy Spirit in our lives, every place we go with Him is truly holy ground.

9
Amazing Grace

Limping Through Life, Remembering

In him we have redemption through his blood,
the forgiveness of sins, in accordance with
the riches of God's grace.

—EPHESIANS 1:7

In the mid-1700s an angry sailor threw a whaling harpoon at his drunken captain, who had fallen overboard on the high seas. Captain John Newton was a wicked, loathsome, and cruel taskmaster with little regard for his crew or the human cargo chained in the hold of his slave ship. The harpoon caught Newton in his hip and he was hauled back on board, much like a large fish. The wound caused him to limp for the rest of his life.

John Newton, born in London, England, in 1725, had been going to sea since age ten. His mother, who had carefully educated young John and taught him Scripture passages and hymns, died just prior to his seventh birthday. After spending three years at school, young Newton went to sea with his father, a ship's master. It seemed to be the only way the older Newton knew how to care for his young son.

The hardened sailors aboard his father's ship became Newton's role models. As a result, he grew to be more wretched than almost anyone with whom he associated. His lifestyle led to rebellion, desertion, public floggings, abuse, and destitution, all consequences of his reckless behavior.

As he grew older he joined himself to another ship, becoming an employee of a slave trader. On a trip to Africa, Newton became very ill and was left in the charge of an African woman who despised him, locked him away, and very nearly starved him to death. Only the kindness of the slaves in chains kept him alive, as they shared with him small portions of their limited allotments of food.

Often during those miserable experiences, Newton's thoughts would return to his loving mother and the things she had taught him. He often read from the Bible, especially on Sundays, and afterward would lapse into an even more wicked state. He later confessed that he tried to influence others to join him in his sinful acts and unholy attitudes. While in this condition, Newton seemed to be totally unaware of God's marvelous grace in sparing his life, time and time again.

Because of his years of experience at sea, Newton was made captain of a slave ship while still a very young man. After a frightening experience during a violent storm at sea, when he despaired of his life, Newton began to earnestly seek a right relationship with God. He began reading *Imitation of Christ* by Thomas á Kempis, a book that had a profound influence on his thinking.

The Lord used another harrowing voyage laden with cattle, lumber, and beeswax to cause young Newton to seriously consider his standing before a holy God. After being at sea for several months, the ship ran into a violent storm. So severe was the gale that the otherwise seaworthy vessel was in danger of sinking. After the livestock were washed overboard, the crew tied themselves to parts of the ship to keep from being swept into the sea.

For four weeks the sailors despaired of life. They spent most of their waking hours at the pumps, desperately trying to lighten the ship of water. Rations were so low that the men feared starvation. Newton's terror was heightened by the fact that he could not swim. When they finally reached a port in Ireland, Newton began a sincere effort to become right with God.

Some time later, at age twenty-three, Newton found himself on a small island off the coast of North Africa. He had contracted an illness that left him listless and burning with fever. He wrote, "Weak and almost delirious, I arose from my bed and crept to a secluded part of the island; there I found a renewed liberty to pray. I made no more resolves, but cast myself before the Lord to do with me as He should please. I was enabled to hope and believe in a crucified Savior. The burden was removed from my conscience."

From that hour, according to his autobiography, Newton began to improve, both physically and spiritually. At that time and by God's grace, John Newton began a new life.

Shortly afterward he parked his ship at South Hampton, England, married his sweetheart of several years, and began to study for the ministry. He later became the pastor of a small church in Olney, England, where he stayed and ministered for twenty years. While there he wrote scores of hymns and sacred songs. In 1779, he, with the help of William Cowper, who wrote "There Is a Fountain Filled with Blood," published a collection entitled *The Olney Hymns,* which included the hymn "Amazing Grace." The captivating melody to which the lyrics are sung was written some fifty years later.

> *Amazing grace, how sweet the sound,*
> *that saved a wretch like me.*
> *I once was lost, but now am found,*
> *was blind, but now I see.*
>
> *Through many dangers, toils and snares,*
> *I have already come.*
> *'Tis grace hath brought me safe thus far,*
> *and grace will lead me home.*
>
> *'Twas grace that taught my heart to fear,*
> *and grace my fears relieved.*
> *How precious did that grace appear,*
> *the hour I first believed.*

Newton later confessed, "Each limp is a constant reminder of God's grace to this wretched sinner." He passed away on December 21, 1807, at age eighty-two, but not before writing his own epitaph, which included the following description:

> *John Newton, clerk,*
> *once an infidel and libertine,*
> *a servant of slaves in Africa,*
> *was by the rich mercy of*
> *our Lord and Savior, Jesus Christ,*
> *preserved, restored, pardoned*
> *and appointed to preach the faith he had long*
> *labored to destroy.*

REFLECTION:
Anyone who reads the above story can see in it the grace of Christ extended to John Newton. Our need for grace is as great as Newton's, and amazingly, we can experience the same miraculous conversion afforded him.

10
Change My Heart, O God

Dictation at a Traffic Signal

Create in me a clean heart, O God;
and renew a steadfast spirit within me. . . . Restore to me the joy of
Your salvation, and uphold me by Your generous Spirit.

—PSALM 51:10, 12

When God wants to give a song, it doesn't matter where the songwriter is or what he or she is doing—the lyrics and melody seem to come all at once, as quickly as they can be put on paper. Such was the experience of Eddie Espinosa when God gave him the song "Change My Heart, O God."

Eddie was born in Los Angeles, one of four brothers. The Espinosa household was always filled with different kinds of music. Eddie's dad loved *The Lawrence Welk Show,* especially Myron Floren and his accordion. Consequently, Eddie started accordion lessons as a young child. That lasted about four years, until the Beatles came on the scene with their guitars.

At age fifteen, Eddie was playing in a high school-age band when the bass player invited Eddie to his church. On Eddie's third visit, the pastor taught about Jesus' encounter with the Samaritan woman at the well. After the lesson, the pastor asked Eddie, "Would you like to drink of the Living Water?" Eddie eagerly agreed, and he was saved that morning.

Eddie's popular worship song "Change My Heart, O God" was written in 1982. Although Eddie had been a Christian for many years, he was beginning to see a lot of things in his life that needed to be discarded. Eddie explains, "The closer you get to the Lord, in all of His brightness, the better you can see the things in your life that need to be changed. I was like Paul, the apostle, who said, 'O wretched man that I am! Who shall deliver me?' I prayed, 'Lord, the only way that I can follow You is for You to change my appetite, the things that draw me away. You must change my heart!"

Shortly after his prayer, Eddie was in his car on the way to work, feeling a desire to draw near to God but still unsettled in his heart. Suddenly, words and a melody began to flood through his mind. As he stopped at a traffic signal, he grabbed a small piece of yellow paper and began to write as rapidly as he could. "It was like taking dictation," Eddie recalls. "I wrote the words on the paper and kept the melody in my mind." The essence of Eddie's song is a prayer asking God to change us, making our hearts "true" and molding us into His own image.

During those days Eddie taught a home Bible study group from Vineyard Christian Fellowship in Anaheim, California, and during a communion time he shared the song God had given him. Someone from the group mentioned to the pastor that Eddie had written a song that would be good to use during an altar call. The pastor asked Eddie if he would share "Change My Heart, O God" with the congregation, which numbered about two hundred at that time. Soon after, Eddie began to get reports that his song was being taught in San Diego, the Los Angeles area, and in many other places. Sharing a song in that manner was a common occurrence in those days. Vineyard decided to include "Change My Heart, O God" on an album of worship songs, which launched the song to a vast audience.

Eddie has had many great experiences with his song, one of which occurred while he was in England directing music for a conference. After one of the services he was standing on the floor level in front of the podium, when an elderly gentleman approached him and asked, "Are you Eddie Espinosa?" He replied, "Yes sir."

The man hugged Eddie, weeping, and said through his tears, "I just want you to know that I gave my heart to Jesus while singing your song. My wife wanted me to go to church for a long time. I finally consented to go, and as the words of your song came up on the overhead I read them and began to weep. As we sang the song, I joined in the singing with real meaning in my heart. I said, 'God, I need You. Change me.' That is the reason I am walking with the Lord today."

Eddie currently works as a counselor at Orange High School in

Orange, California. He also oversees a federally funded program for children. He has written scores of songs, with thirty-eight of them being published. As his other duties allow, Eddie and his wife, Else, often travel as a team, leading worship in conferences and special services. The Espinosas and their two children are active in Vineyard Christian Fellowship.

REFLECTION:
Asking God to change us calls for a very definite and resolute decision—asking Him to change our hearts, the control center of our beings. When we admit our need for God, He comes to us and transforms what we think, say, and do into the things that are pleasing to Him.

11
My Life Is in You, Lord

He Was Pressed, Then Blessed

Your life is hidden with Christ in God.
When Christ who is our life appears,
then you also will appear with Him in glory.

—COLOSSIANS 3:3–4

Dan Gardner was really bushed one Sunday afternoon. He knew he needed something, but he had no idea that God was about to give him something he couldn't keep. Dan just had to share it with others. And to this date he has kept sharing it, and sharing it, until his generosity has gone around the world and back to him again.

Dan is a preacher's kid who came to know the Lord at an early age. His parents founded the church where Dan is presently the worship leader at Zion Christian Church in Troy, Michigan. He is one of four children, all of whom are musical. Dan plays piano, guitar, and trumpet, using his ability to play instruments to the fullest during the services. He began his songwriting ventures as a teenager with a song he titled "Praise Ye the Lord."

Dan wrote "My Life Is in You, Lord" in the mid-1980s, when he, his wife, Joanne, and their two daughters were living at Joanne's parents' home while their house was being built. Dan was very busy in those days, raising a family, going to college full-time, and serving as the full-time worship leader at Zion Church.

On Sunday afternoon, after leading the worship for two Sunday morning services, Dan sat down to do some homework for his college music composition class. He barely had time enough to complete the assignment and still prepare to lead the worship in the evening service.

Dan recalls feeling pressed by the hands of the clock and desperately needing added energy. He knew it would help him if he would relax and wait on God. So he sat down at the piano and began to play and sing to the Lord, as he often had done during such times. As he was worshiping God in this manner, suddenly from his heart came the words, "My life is in You, Lord." The words and a melody kept coming quickly until Dan had the entire song.

"As one of the Lord's worship leaders, I have sought to find that place of abandoning the control of my life to Him," admits Dan. "I am still learning to trust Him completely. I know that when I do, He graces me with the strength of His presence in my life. I know that I cannot glorify Him with my life apart from the power of His Spirit to do so."

Zion Church published "My Life Is in You, Lord" in 1985, and some time later Integrity Music recorded it on a project featuring Joseph Garlington, after which the song began to have a wide audience.

To date, Dan has written more than two hundred songs, with approximately fifty of them published, including "Exalt the Lord, Our God" and "Blessed Be the Rock." He feels blessed to see such a proliferation of songwriters in the praise and worship movement. He says, "It is difficult to keep up with all of the great material coming our way—a wonderful outpouring!"

REFLECTION:

Can you think of anything more comforting than to realize that our very beings are engulfed in the heavenly Father, through His precious Son? As the song says, God gives us "life" and "strength" and "hope," and in return we praise Him with all of our lives.

12
Jesus, Name above All Names

From the Washhouse to the World

Therefore God also has highly exalted Him
and given Him the name which is above every name.

—PHILIPPIANS 2:9

Naida Hearn never dreamed that she would influence Christian singing around the world, but she has done just that. Born in Palmerston North, New Zealand in 1931, Naida attended Sunday school as a young child and began to learn the things of the Bible. Those biblical truths became increasingly dear to her as she continued her life in the quiet, peaceful town in the north of her island nation.

Of the approximately twelve songs she wrote, only one has been published—but what a song it is! As Naida was nearing her fortieth birthday, she was studying the Bible and became interested in the different names referring to Jesus. So great was her interest that she began to make a list of the names on a piece of paper.

As is the case with many homes in her neighborhood, her family had a "washhouse" behind the regular living quarters of the home. One day in the early 1970s as she made her way to the washhouse, she carried with her the paper on which she had written the names of Jesus and placed it on the windowsill. The paper was in full view as she did the washing.

Feeling in a very worshipful mood, Naida began to sing. While she was doing the washing, the Lord gave her the first line, "Jesus, name above all names." So Naida began singing, and she sang the whole chorus just as we sing it today.

Naida remembers thinking, *Well, I'll write it down*. She left the washing, went down to the piano in the sitting room, and wrote out the chorus on manuscript paper. After she finished, she asked, "Lord, is that okay? Is it all right like that?" She felt God saying that yes, it was all right. Said Naida, "That was all I wrote, and then I went back to the washing. It was just that simple. It was a straight-out lead from the Holy Spirit, absolutely. I can't say I thought about this or I thought about that; I just started on 'Jesus, name above all names' and it carried on all by itself."

Soon after, the chorus was sung in her church, New Life Church in Palmerton North. Visitors from other parts of her country who attended the church service took the chorus to their churches. Missionaries began to carry it overseas, where it quickly became a favorite. Soon "Jesus, Name above All Names" was being sung in several nations.

"I've had all sorts of people write to me asking that I add three more verses," Naida said. "But if the Lord had wanted three more verses He would have given them to me. All that needed to be said was said. The Spirit impressed on me that it was to be sung as a love song. It's all about Him. You are supposed to sing it softly, slowly and reverently, as if He were our lover. This is what He wanted."

"Jesus, Name above All Names" continues to be one of the most popular praise choruses in the world today. It always ranks very high on the list of songs most requested and sung in churches. It has been published in a number of songbooks and hymnals and has been recorded on numerous occasions.

In April 2001, Naida left this earth to be with the One whose name is above all names, her glorious Lord through so many of her seventy years.

REFLECTION:

As you consider the names given to our Savior, you too will be drawn closer to Him. As Naida suggested, sing "Jesus, Name above All Names" very softly as a love song to Him.

13
Majesty

A Monarch's Celebration Inspires a Song

When He had by Himself purged our sins,
He sat down at the right hand of the Majesty on high.

——HEBREWS 1:3

Dr. Jack Hayford, for many years pastor of the Church on the Way in Van Nuys, California, is not only an outstanding preacher and Bible teacher, but also a talented songwriter. The composition that has brought him the most acclaim has a rather unusual history.

Years ago, Dr. and Mrs. Hayford traveled for ten days in Denmark, where he had speaking engagements. Following their stay in Denmark, they took advantage of two weeks of free time before another scheduled series of meetings in Oxford, England.

The year was the silver anniversary of the coronation of Elizabeth II as queen of England. The celebrating, countryside, and spirit of enthusiasm of the English people, coupled with the great historical significance of that nation, made those two weeks a very special time for the Hayfords. Dr. Hayford reports that he was completely caught up in the emotion of the occasion. As he walked among the people and saw signs of history on every corner, he sensed a feeling of grandeur and nobility. While touring the countryside, the couple made a short visit to Blenheim, the palace where Winston Churchill grew up and where he would occasionally go aside for a short rest during the horrors of World War II.

Although that monumental chapter of history was a generation past, stories of those days came rushing back to Pastor Hayford. As he looked around, he sensed that even though individuals are greatly used in the course of man's existence on this earth, there is a greater power to be honored, the One who is the Author of our destiny.

As he felt the courage and motivation of the English people, Dr. Hayford realized that they also had a profound respect and love for the royalty who stood with them in dark hours. Even now they were excited about sharing in the celebration of their monarch. Dr. Hayford began to consider that Christ wants His church to have such a sense of loyalty and fellowship, because He must be our leader in good times and bad.

Standing on the magnificent, well-groomed landscape surrounding Blenheim Palace, Dr. Hayford said to his wife, "Honey, I can hardly describe to you all the things that this setting evokes in me. There is something of majesty in all this, and I believe it has a great deal to do with why people who lived here have been of such consequence in the shaping of history. I don't mean that building and beauty can beget greatness, but I do feel that some people fail to perceive their possibilities because of their dismal surroundings."

As he shared with her how Christ wants to exercise His kingdom authority in our lives and our being, one word seemed to charge to the forefront: *majesty*. The word seemed at the moment to represent the glory, excellence, grace, and power of Christ. By comparison, Queen Elizabeth seemed but a paltry reminder of the royal heritage we enjoy as we worship the majesty of our risen Lord.

While they drove away from that regal palace, Dr. Hayford asked his wife to take a notebook and write down a few words. He then began to dictate the key, the notes, the timing, and the lyrics to one of the most popular new songs now being used by Christians worldwide—"Majesty."

Dr. Hayford draws together his knowledge of the meaning of "worship" in this magnificent song. The theme of the song begins in the second line, ascribing to Jesus all "glory," "honor," and "praise," and ends with the great biblical title, "King of all kings." The song was edited and completed some time later at the piano in Dr. Hayford's living room. Never in their wildest dreams could the Hayfords have imagined the impact that this song would have on the singing of Christians in so many lands.

"Majesty" has been used in musicals, in youth rallies, in concerts, and in church congregational singing. You would be hard-pressed to find an adult, teen, or child attending church services who does not know it. Just as Christians eagerly proclaim Christ as Lord and Master, just so this song is sung enthusiastically wherever Christians meet to praise the Lord.

REFLECTION:

When we see the great King and are face to face with His glory, we will be overjoyed to forever adore His majesty and His power. While we wait, we bow to His authority as we "lift up on high the name of Jesus."

14
His Name Is Wonderful

A Christmas Long Remembered

For unto us a Child is born, unto us a Son is given; and the government will be upon His shoulder. And His name will be called Wonderful, Counselor, Mighty God, Everlasting Father, Prince of Peace.

—Isaiah 9:6

Although Audrey Mieir is now with her heavenly Father, her songs live on in the hearts of Christians everywhere. She was not only a great composer, but also a marvelous organist, pianist, and choral director.

Audrey directed very talented choral groups, such as the Phil Kerr Singers, and served in small churches as well. It was in one of those small churches that her most famous song was written. It happened on Christmas Day, which that year happened to fall on a Sunday.

That year, the congregation of Bethel Union Church in Duarte, California, had decided that they would feature their young people in the annual Christmas pageant. Mary was a teenage girl, and the angels were young boys. The baby was a doll.

The angels' halos were a little crooked and the shepherds' pants were rolled up under their dads' bathrobes, but something wonderful was about to take place.

The entire church smelled of pine boughs, and the atmosphere was so expectant that Audrey recalled that she could almost hear the rustling of angels' wings. To her, the whole room seemed to be filled with the presence of the angels of God.

Audrey looked down as little children were listening thoughtfully to the soft organ music and the older people were wiping away tears, remembering Christmases gone by. Then the pastor stood up and lifted his hands toward heaven, exclaiming, "His name is Wonderful!" Audrey recalls, "Those words electrified me. I immediately began writing in the back of my Bible. As I wrote, I was thinking that God has something He wants said. I wrote a simple chorus and sang it that night for the young people around the piano. They sang it immediately. It wasn't hard for them to learn. I never dreamed that it would go any further, but it has traveled around the world in many languages." She gave God all of the praise and glory for using her to give the world such a praise chorus.

Some time later, Audrey met music publisher Tim Spencer, who told her that she had written a good song, but it needed a bridge. At that time Audrey didn't know what he meant. He explained to her that she could cause the song to be much more of a blessing with an extension to the chorus she had written. So she opened her Bible, reviewed some names of Christ in the concordance, and wrote them down on a napkin. Later, in her office, she finished the song.

The song uses a number of different names given to Christ in the Bible, such as "Wonderful," "Lord," "King," "Master," "Great Shepherd," "Rock," "Almighty God," and "Jesus." The thrice-repeated phrase, "His name is Wonderful," sets the tone and the spirit of the song as it should be sung.

How thankful we should be that God chose Aubrey Mieir to use her talents to praise Him with this simple and powerful song.

REFLECTION:

Why not make this song meaningful in your life today? Make the Lord Jesus Christ your Great Shepherd to lead your every step, the Rock on which you rest secure, and the Master of every area of your life.

15
Give Thanks

What a Song!

[Give] thanks always for all things to God the Father
in the name of our Lord Jesus Christ,
submitting to one another in the fear of God.

—Ephesians 5:20–21

In Uzbekistan, a country just north of the war-torn land of Afghanistan, a group of Uzbekies gather together and begin to sing a Christian song they recently learned. This is an unusual sight in a country that is a mixture of Soviet industrial atheism, Islam, and the Orient. The group is singing Henry Smith's "Give Thanks," which has traveled from America to this place.

Other stories, perhaps not as unusual but heartwarming to say the least, can be told of the blessing that this song has been to Christians during the past thirty years. The popularity of the song has been dramatic and even unprecedented at times.

Henry Smith, Jr., was born in Crossnore, North Carolina. He started piano lessons at age seven but wanted no part of that. In his early teens, however, he picked up his brother's guitar and learned how to play it by reading the instruction manual. Henry's song-writing ventures started during those early years and have lasted until the present. Of the nearly three hundred songs he has written, only one has been published.

While Henry was a sophomore at King College in Bristol, Tennessee, the Lord seemed to increase His blessings as He poured out His Spirit upon Henry. "Music for me has not been the same since that time," he says. "I only wanted to write songs for Christ." Henry started putting psalms to music, which revitalized his songwriting.

Six years later, in an apartment in Williamsburg, Virginia, he wrote the song, "Give Thanks." At the Williamsburg New Testament Church, where he attended, the pastor had taught from the Scripture how Jesus became poor in order that we might be made rich in Him. Henry thought that the teaching would be a good background for a song.

Shortly thereafter, Henry and his future wife, Cindy, sang the song at the church and repeated it a number of times during a period of several weeks. Henry recalls, "There happened to be a military couple who attended the church for a while who carried songs learned in the United States back with them to Germany. As far as I know that is how my song got to Europe. It did a lot of traveling before Integrity Music published it. It is a 'God thing' that the song took off as it did."

In 1986, eight years after Henry wrote the song, a friend brought him a cassette tape and said, "Listen to this song and see if you have ever heard it." After listening to it, Henry exclaimed, "I wrote that song!" His friend had ordered the Hosanna! tape from Integrity Music, and "Give Thanks" was listed as "author unknown." Henry immediately called Integrity and told them that he had written the song. They gladly responded, "Good! We have been trying to find you," and gave Henry a writer-publisher agreement. Now more than fifty companies have recorded the song, and it has been published in a number of songbooks.

A few years later, the Smiths attended a live Integrity Music recording session in Washington, D.C. During the session, Don Moen played a recording that featured Henry's song being sung in Russian. Henry recalls, "My wife and I began to weep. We were overwhelmed to hear my song in that language. Moen had no idea we were in the audience."

For five or six years "Give Thanks" has been in the top ten of Christian Copyright Licensing International's Top 25 list of songs used by churches in the United States, reaching as high as second and third. Many people worldwide love this song because the "weak" can sing "I am strong!," and the "poor" can say "I am rich!," for the all-encompassing reason: "because of what the Lord has done for us."

Henry is now preparing to record a CD commemorating his thirty years of writing Christian songs. Since 1996, Henry has owned Christian Media Resources and is also the proprietor of the

Outback Studio. He is also a worship leader at the Mechanicsville Christian Center. Henry and Cindy have two children and reside in Mechanicsville, Virginia.

REFLECTION:

Every good thing that we possess is a gift from our heavenly Father. Let us joyfully acknowledge the generosity our heavenly Father and give Him thanks for all the things He has done for us.

16
Awesome God

A Ragamuffin Band

Let all the earth fear the LORD;
let all the inhabitants of the world stand in awe of Him.

—PSALM 33:8

The scene was the Ryman Auditorium in Nashville, Tennessee. A great crowd had gathered for the opening of the Gospel Music Association's annual convention in 1995, awaiting many of the most popular performers in contemporary Christian music. Each person on the program presented his or her musical offering accompanied by beautiful lighting and special effects. After several performances, a man walked onto the stage and took his place at the piano with a choir behind him. As the lights were going up, Rich Mullins began to play, some thought somewhat prematurely. Unshaven and dressed in scruffy jeans and a flannel shirt, Rich scarcely looked up from the piano as he played his signature song, "Awesome God." When he was finished, the music ceased, the lights went down, and Rich Mullins slipped away—out of sight. Such was the humility of this man.

Let me say before I go any further with this chapter that I do not have the facts surrounding the writing of Rich Mullins's song "Awesome God." After a tragic automobile accident, Rich went home to be with the Lord on September 19, 1997, before I could get his story. But Rich's extensive contributions to contemporary praise and worship music compels me to include this chapter.

Michael W. Smith had this to say about his friend: "Rich Mullins's life and music have impacted me more than anyone I know. He had the ability to take the mundane and make it majestic. Nobody on this planet wrote songs like he did, and I feel we've lost one of the only true poets in our industry. I love Rich Mullins. No one will ever know how much I'll miss him."

Rich was born into a Quaker home in a small community near Richmond, Indiana. The people in his community called him Wayne, for fear of confusing him with his Uncle Richard Mullins, who loaned him the money to make his first album. Rich's parents recognized that he showed a tremendous music ability early in life. One day when he was about five years of age, his mother said that Rich was in the room listening to his older sister, Debbie, practice her piano lesson. She became very frustrated after trying several times to play a song without making mistakes. In desperation she left the room. Young Rich climbed onto the piano bench and played the song perfectly. Mrs. Mullins, listening from another room, complimented Debbie on finally getting it right.

As a youngster attending the Quaker church, Rich's opinion of some of the music of the church was less than complimentary. He thought the poetry and the musical settings were poor. It was not until he saw the effect the music had on people he respected that he changed his mind.

Rich attended the Cincinnati Bible College and while there formed a band called Zion, which played local engagements. He later became a major recording artist and formed a band to tour with him called The Ragamuffin Band, including musicians Rick Elias, Jimmy Abegg, Mark Robertson, and Aaron Smith. During Rich's brief music career, he was nominated for twelve Dove Awards.

Rich Mullins loved poor children and spent his money for causes that benefited them. He lived the last two years of his life on the Navajo Indian Reservation near the Arizona–New Mexico border, working with poor Native Americans. He believed that music was the language of the soul, and he wanted to give this gift to the children.

I also learned from his "Uncle Dick," as Rich called him, that during the last years of Rich's life, although he could have lived sumptuously, he allowed himself a yearly wage of only $27,000, the average wage for a man in the U.S. The rest of his money went to a foundation to help the children. He named the foundation Kid Brother of St. Frank, after a thirteenth-century churchman, St. Francis of Assisi, who lived a life of denial to self. Rich's mother is making sure that the money Rich left behind goes to the causes he loved so dearly.

So the next time you sing "Awesome God," may it be as meaningful to you as it was to its author.

REFLECTION:

May you and I recognize that in everything our heavenly Father is omnipotent, omniscient, and omnipresent. His majesty, power, and might are far beyond our ability to comprehend. Yet this great God invites you and me to fellowship with Him, offering us eternal life in His presence.

17
Because He Lives

A Sudden Calm and Peaceful Rest

A little while longer and the world will see Me no more,
but you will see Me. Because I live, you will live also.

—JOHN 14:19

Who among us has not seen one of the Gaither Homecoming concerts on television or viewed a *Homecoming* video, the sales of which number into the millions? Thousands flock to these live concerts, which are videotaped in scores of cities across America. By producing the Homecoming concerts and videos, Bill and Gloria Gaither have exposed millions of Americans to southern gospel music and at the same time have shared many praise and worship songs that have come from their prolific and talented pens.

For more than four decades, the Gaithers have touched the lives of multiplied millions around the world. Together they have written and published hundreds of songs, many of which are favorites among Christians.

In the late 1960s, while expecting their third child, Bill and

Gloria Gaither were going through a rather traumatic time. Bill was recovering his strength from a bout with mononucleosis. The Gaithers, along with their church family, were the objects of false accusation and belittlement. Gloria was experiencing a time of torment, including fear of the future and of bringing children into such a crazy, mixed-up world.

On New Years' Eve she sat alone in her darkened living room, agonizing and fearful. She worried about the drug culture running wild, the racial tension spreading across the nation, and the "God is dead" idea making its way into the educational system. But the wonderful God that Gloria serves, who was watching her like a mother bending over her baby, suddenly brought to His "child" a sweet and peaceful rest. Her panic gave place to a calm that surpassed all understanding—an assurance that the future would be fine, left in God's hands. This experience led her to pen the words to "Because He Lives."

As the Gaithers composed the song, the presence of the Holy Spirit was particularly precious as they remembered that His strength and power were at their disposal. The power of the resurrection of Christ seemed to affirm itself in their lives again. Gloria realized that "it was life conquering death in the regularity of my day." Joy overcame her fear and took precedence over her troubling circumstances.

In her book *Fully Alive,* Gloria recalls another experience of

God's affirmation to her that His life would conquer any circumstance, even death. One day in the late fall, the Gaithers hired workers to pave the parking lot behind their office. The workers brought load after load of coarse rocks, pea gravel, and sand. Then they brought huge, heavy rollers and smashed all of that down. Again and again they rolled it. Finally came the steaming truckloads of molten asphalt to be poured atop the gravel, then rolled again and again until it was smooth and hard and permanent.

Very early the next spring, Bill's dad came into the office one morning and stood around on first one foot, then the other, grinning as if he had something special on his mind. "Come out here," he finally said to Bill and Gloria. They followed him out the back door onto the shining new pavement. Right in the middle of it he stopped and pointed, "Look, there."

Up through the sand, up through the gravel, up through the rocks, up from the darkness and through the thick layer of asphalt had pushed a green shoot. It wasn't tough, it wasn't sharp, and it wasn't strong. Any child could have plucked it up with practically no effort. But it was alive! And there it stood, bright green in the sunlight, boasting to the world of its photosynthetic miracle: *Life* wins!

Recalls Gloria, "There wasn't much to say. We just smiled our message of reassurance at each other; but I couldn't help thinking of the song we had just written after our own personal bout with darkness."

The first verse of "Because He Lives" is a presentation of the gospel of Christ, reminding us of His death, burial, and resurrection. Then the second verse pictures the life of a newborn baby and assures us that this little one can have a victorious life, because Christ lives.

We can face tomorrow, with all of the uncertainty that it brings, as we realize that God holds the future and makes life worth living for all who trust in Him.

REFLECTION:

The awareness and the assurance of the Savior's resurrection gives strength to overcome the frightening obstacles of life—because He lives, every single day, in our hearts.

18
More Precious Than Silver

The Heartache of a Broken Fast

*Receive my instruction, and not silver, and knowledge
rather than choice gold; for wisdom is better than rubies,
and all the things one may desire cannot be compared with her.*

—PROVERBS 8:10–11

Lynn DeShazzo, a prolific composer of praise choruses, developed a love for music at an early age, learning to play the guitar by age eleven. In her teen years she wanted desperately to improve her music ability and tried to do so by playing her guitar along with songs she heard on the radio. Although she yielded her heart to Christ before reaching her twelfth birthday, praise and worship music did not have a great deal of meaning to her until much later.

In her first year at Auburn University in Auburn, Alabama, she developed a desire to write Christian songs—songs that would be expressions of her heart to the Lord and meaningful to people who heard them. Those first efforts at songwriting were seemingly quite meager, yet people responded very positively. She was greatly encouraged by their attitudes toward her first unpublished songs.

After Lynn graduated with a degree in recreation administration, she took a job at McDonald's—not the most likely place for an Auburn alumnus to work, yet it provided for her livelihood during the first months following graduation. During this time, Lynn learned valuable spiritual lessons as she continued her involvement with a campus church at Auburn called Maranatha Ministries.

After learning that Christians should occasionally fast and that fasting was a scriptural method of spiritual growth, Lynn found herself one Wednesday in a precarious situation. Her boss at McDonald's had assigned her to the task of cooking French fries on a day of fasting for her. Well, needless to say, the battle was on!

Lynn recalls that the fries smelled oh, so good! As the day wore on, her hunger made the idea of breaking her fast by eating only a couple of French fries pale into insignificance. After looking around to make sure that no one would see her, she slipped a few fries into her mouth. At that moment she was almost overcome with guilt—guilt that was twofold: She knew that she had broken her fast and that she had done it with stolen French fries.

After work that day, and as soon as she could get alone with the Lord, she earnestly asked His forgiveness for breaking her fast and for taking something that did not belong to her. She was led to Colossians 2:3, where she found that in Christ are the hidden "treasures of wisdom and knowledge." She also went to Proverbs 8, which reveals that there are spiritual things that are of more value than silver and gold or precious jewels, and the earthly things we often desire cannot be compared with them.

Lynn began to play her guitar, and the Lord dropped a song into her heart. At that moment she felt so blessed. As the guilt had been twofold, so too was the blessing. She was overtaken with the joy of God's forgiveness and the excitement of His gift—a beautiful song.

She shared "More Precious Than Silver" with the worship leader of her campus church, who rejoiced in it and used it in subsequent worship services. She related how he had been a great encouragement and had urged her to continue in her songwriting.

Her song soon began to be sung in other places, such as Christ for the Nations Institute in Dallas, Texas. The students loved it and began sharing it in services where they had opportunity to minister. It soon was being sung far and wide. "More Precious Than Silver" was published by Integrity Music in 1982 and presented on their recording *Glory to the King* in 1986. It has since been translated into several languages and continues to be sung around the world, ranking very high on the list of popular praise choruses.

In 1981, Lynn moved to Ann Arbor, Michigan, were she worked with the Information Services Department of the University of Michigan Medical School. She returned to Birmingham in the fall of 1989, and since that time has served with Integrity Music as a staff writer. She continues to write songs and to travel as a guest worship leader in churches, conferences, and women's ministries.

She has written more than three hundred songs, many of which appear in several music books and collections of choral arrangements. To date she has produced seven recordings of her own music. Other popular songs she has written include, "Be Glorified," "Lead Me to the Rock," and "In Your Presence, O God." When Lynn is not on the road ministering in other cities, she is very active on the worship team in her home church, Liberty Church in Hoover, Alabama, a suburb of Birmingham.

REFLECTION:

When things seem to be going a bit sideways, examine yourself to see if the greatest longing of your heart compares with the One who is more precious than silver, more costly than gold, and more beautiful than diamonds. You might also check your heart to see if there is anything you desire that, in your estimation, compares with Him.

19
Seek Ye First

From the Nightclubs to the Mission Fields

Seek ye first the kingdom of God and His righteousness,
and all these things shall be added to you.

—MATTHEW 6:33

Karen Lafferty is one of the pioneers of contemporary Christian music. She was writing songs in that genre before she knew that a few others were doing the same. But it took her awhile to become a part of the mainstream. Karen is a master musician and shares her Christian faith by singing and speaking in the farthest places on our planet. She has an extremely varied background, the experiences of which the Lord now uses in her ministry.

During Karen's early childhood, her parents took her to the local Southern Baptist church in Alamogordo, New Mexico. She started lessons on piano at six, saxophone at nine, guitar at twelve, and oboe, which was to become a part of her college degree, at age thirteen. She attended Eastern New Mexico University, graduating with a degree in choral music and oboe.

She made a commitment to Christ at age eleven, but in college Karen began to drift from the Lord. Her childhood friend Rhonda Ray was involved with Campus Crusade for Christ and had become a dedicated, vibrant Christian. Karen soon wanted to have what her friend had. In early 1971, Rhonda showed Karen one of the tracts from CCC, "Have You Made the Wonderful Discovery of the Spirit-Filled Life?"

After reading the tract, Karen realized that she had ego and ambitions, not Jesus Christ, on the throne of her life. Says Karen, "I was faced with a strong decision, I said, 'OK, I'm not going to be a hypocrite about this. I'm going to live for Christ or I'm not.'" Karen found she had learned to put on three faces: one for her family, one for the church, and another for the clubs. She truly felt like a hypocrite.

She was entertaining in New Orleans when she made the life-changing decision to make Christ Lord of her life. She then learned about a Christian music conference in California with Campus Crusade for Christ and jumped at the chance to attend, since she was seeking to know how she could best use her music for God. There she saw people using contemporary Christian music in ministry and felt that God could be calling her to pursue a career as a singer and songwriter so that she could better influence her generation for Christ.

She moved to California with this motive in her prayers. Aware that the hippie drug culture had much of its roots in that state, she prayed, "God, please lead me to some Christians and a church where I can grow." The second day she was there, she attended Calvary Chapel in Costa Mesa, which became her church home. She met other young musicians who met together regularly for Bible study, worship, and planning concerts and recordings. The group later became known as Maranatha Music.

Learning about ministry at Calvary Chapel and being part of the Maranatha Music fellowship was very exciting, and Karen knew she was in the right place. In those days there were very few models of full-time contemporary Christian music ministry, and many Christian musicians had to work other jobs. Karen knew God wanted her in full-time music ministry, but she worried about what she was going to do about her bills. So she began to sing at churches and coffee houses where she would receive honorariums, but it just wasn't enough.

During this stressful and unhappy period in her life, Karen attended a Monday night youth Bible study. The subject that night was Matthew 6. The lesson emphasized that we as God's people should "seek first" the kingdom of God and His righteousness and all of these other "things" would be added unto us. Karen believed God's Word and went home happy. "The bills still weren't paid," she admits, "but I had my joy back."

At home after the study, Karen began to pluck around on the

guitar and came up with a melody that closely fit with the passage she had studied that night. She finished writing the song and went to bed happy about it.

The following Monday evening Karen taught "Seek Ye First" to the Bible study group. The melody was so memorable that it quickly spread to other Bible study classes. During that time Maranatha Music was doing its first praise album, which became the forerunner to all of the praise albums in the Maranatha series. Karen sang "Seek Ye First" as a duet with Ernie Rettino and even played her oboe as part of the background music.

Since that time, Karen's song has literally gone around the world, being sung in many languages. The royalties from the chorus now help pay for her many trips abroad as she continues to teach others about the goodness of God through the ministry of music.

For more than two decades Karen has concentrated her energies on developing Musicians for Missions, International. She has led many multinational teams on tours in more than fifty countries, held numerous music seminars and short-term outreaches for musicians, launched a School of Music in Missions as part of Youth with a Mission's University of the Nations, and produced or assisted in many recordings in several languages.

REFLECTION:

Karen learned one of the most difficult lessons in the Bible for Christians to absorb: We cannot outgive God. He is more anxious to give us the things we need than we can ever imagine. His plan is simple: If we seek first God's kingdom and His righteousness, He adds to us all the "things" that we need.

20
He Has Made Me Glad

It Started in the Appalachian Mountains

For You, LORD, have made me glad through Your work;
I will triumph in the works of Your hands.

—PSALM 92:4

If you had driven through the majestic Appalachian mountain range six or seven decades ago, you would have seen breathtaking sights that would have compelled you to reach for your camera. But if you had gotten off the beaten paths and into the backwoods of this vast stretch of seeming grandeur, you would have discovered pockets of poverty unparalleled in our nation. Not only did those who endured the pains of privation find themselves in dire circumstances, they were also far removed from those who might render aid.

Those were the circumstances in which the Bruce family found themselves in the early 1920s. Leona was one of eleven children born to this fearful, deprived family, yet she would be used of the Lord to give a song of joy and happiness to the people of the world.

Leona's family was "land poor," and they lived much like the pioneers, with no plumbing or electricity. They grew their own food, which, in those mountains, came at the cost of hard labor. Leona and her family worked long hours just to survive. To make matters worse, her father was a strict disciplinarian who severely disciplined his children for the smallest matter that caused him displeasure.

As a small, sensitive child, Leona developed a spirit of fear that shaped her life. Her father, who never hugged or displayed any affection toward his children, once saw Leona sucking her thumb and threatened to cut it off with his razor. It frightened young Leona almost beyond words.

Leona and her family often lacked proper clothes for the cruel winters in the Appalachian Mountains. She recalls going barefoot to school on frosty mornings. She and her sisters would often sew pasteboard together in an effort to make shoes so they could play outside. Leona's mother, a godly woman, was the children's only source of encouragement.

After Leona graduated from high school, she made her way to the factories of Detroit, Michigan, to make a living. She spent three years in the defense plants and from there went on to college to train to be a beautician. She moved to California and, after a short engagement, married Robert Von Brethorst, with whom she had two children, a son and a daughter. Sadly, Robert left the family when the oldest was not yet three years of age. His only financial contribution to their survival was some rent money. Leona was once again thrown into a state of fear and depression, not knowing how she would be able to care for her children.

Leona's son became very ill, and during the sickness she bargained with God by saying, "God, if You will heal my child, I'll give You the rest of my life." The Lord healed her son, and Leona was delivered from the spirit of fear. Not long after that she was called into a ministry of prayer, which she still participates in to this day.

After her children were grown, Leona began to write songs and poems and spend a great deal of time in prayer and fasting. Songs seemed to come easily during those times. One day, after reading 2 Chronicles 5:11–14, where the glory of the Lord came down into the midst of the children of Israel during the dedication of the temple, she prayed, "Lord, if You would do that for a people who were still under the Old Testament law, what would happen if we had the Holy Spirit in our lives?" She then prayed, according to Psalm 100, "Lord, I will enter Your gates with thanksgiving in my heart, and go into Your courts with praise. This is the day You have made, and I will rejoice, for You are well able to prepare for us whatever we need."

Shortly after that, Leona sang the song she had written during that experience to her Sunday school class at Bethany Chapel. As she did so, Leona recalls, "I felt the whole of me was being lifted." Her song "He Has Made Me Glad" has now encouraged thousands of Christians around the world.

Leona never learned to play any kind of musical instrument. Doug Hamblin, an organist at her church, wrote out the music for her so that she could present it to a publisher. Maranatha Music published her song and has seen it bless the hearts of millions of Christians. The royalties that Maranatha Music has sent to Leona have provided much of her living expenses during the past quarter century.

Although Leona has written more than twenty other songs, at the time of this interview, "He Has Made Me Glad" is the only one that has ever been published. For several years, the song was consistently in the top ten songs of the Christian Copyright Licensing International's Top 25 list of songs in America.

Leona is still engaged in her prayer ministry. She now attends City of the Cross Church in Long Beach, California, and has dreams and hopes that the Lord might use another of her songs to bless the hearts of others.

REFLECTION:
In 2 Chronicles 5, when the children of Israel lifted their voices to praise and thank the Lord, then and only then did He manifest His glory in their presence. When we praise God in a spirit of thankfulness, we will be in fellowship with those around us and right with our heavenly Father.

21
Sweet, Sweet Spirit

Not Ready to Go In

The effective, fervent prayer of a righteous man avails much.

—JAMES 5:16

Noted recording artist, music arranger, and director Doris Akers was born in Brookfield, Missouri, and started writing songs at age ten. Many of her more than three hundred songs are found in many songbooks and hymnals and have been sung by millions of worshipers. In addition to songwriting, Doris also founded and directed the Skypilot Choir of Skypilot Church in Los Angeles.

One Sunday morning, Doris said to her choir, "You are not ready to go in." She didn't believe they had prayed enough! They were accustomed to spending time in prayer before the service, asking God to bless their songs. Doris had communicated to her choir that prayer was much more important than great voices. Although the choir members had already prayed this particular morning, she asked them to pray again, and they did so with renewed fervor.

Sweet, Sweet Spirit

As the choir members continued to pray, Doris began to wonder how she could stop this wonderful prayer meeting. She even sent word to the pastor about what was happening. Finally she was compelled to say to the choir, "We have to go. I hate to leave this room and I know you hate to leave, but you know we do have to go to the service. But there is such a sweet, sweet Spirit in this place."

Songwriters always have their ears open to the possibilities of a song, and Doris later recalled that a song started "singing" to her. Since she didn't have time to write it down, she thought the song would be gone after the service. Following the service she went home, and the next morning, to her surprise, she heard the song again, so she went to the piano and began to write, "There's a sweet, sweet Spirit in this place."

In her song she recognized the "Spirit" in the room as the "Spirit of the Lord." She could see in the "sweet expressions" of the choir members that they also recognized the "presence of the Lord." The chorus of the song calls us back to the New Testament's description of the Spirit of God descending like a dove, lighting upon Jesus at His baptism (see Matthew 3:16).

Doris Akers not only wrote songs individually, but also joined her close friend Mahalia Jackson as cowriter in one songwriting venture. In her lifetime she received many awards, one of which was an honor bestowed upon her by the Smithsonian Institute, labeling her songs and records as national treasures.

Doris Akers passed away in 1995, but her songs will live on in the hearts of those of us who have sung them and have learned to love the God she wrote about. Until her last day on earth, Doris strongly believed that God wants His children to pray.

REFLECTION:
Nothing worthwhile has ever been accomplished apart from prayer. How long has it been since you really, really prayed about some need in your life or in the life of a friend or loved one?

22
I Will Glory in the Cross

Fame, Fortune, and Unhappiness

God forbid that I should boast except in the cross of our Lord Jesus Christ,
by whom the world has been crucified to me, and I to the world.

—GALATIANS 6:14

Dottie Rambo once said, "I asked the Lord to let me, at least once each year, write a song that will speak to the hearts of Christians everywhere." Her songs might not have come with that exact frequency, but in the Lord's time He has given to all of us, through her, so many wonderful compositions.

Several years ago, Dottie and her family were doing many competitive concerts, making a lot of money. Suddenly she realized that she was not living close to the Lord or writing under the anointing of the Holy Spirit. She also realized that she had never done anything to merit recognition and fame. Dottie then began to study Galatians 6:14, where Paul said that he didn't glory in himself, but in the cross of Christ. She came to the realization that all she had was only because of the grace of God and the cross of Christ.

In 1978, Dottie's family went to Holland to do a number of concerts. When they got off the plane, people met them and took them to a quaint, little hotel. As they rode along, the escorts informed the Rambos that while they were singing in the concerts, they were not to sing about the cross of Christ. Dottie looked at the young man who was escorting them and asked, "Do you mean we are not allowed to sing about the cross to these Christians?" He said, "No, they consider it gory. They don't want to hear about the blood or the cross." Dottie looked at this young man—she was old enough to be his mother—and said, 'Son, if you won't tell them you told us this, then we will pretend we don't know it. Because we will be singing about the cross and about the blood of Christ."

Dottie's family sang "He Looked Beyond My Fault and Saw My Need" in the concert that very night. People wept all over the audience, including the man who said that they couldn't sing about the cross of Christ. The Lord really seemed to move in the hearts of the people.

Dottie and her family went back to the little hotel that night and to bed. Dottie's husband thought she was asleep, but she began to weep and prayed, "God, I apologize that we are so stupid that we wouldn't want to hear about the blood of Christ, His cross, and His grace." As she lay there in the darkness, the Lord gave her the song, "I Will Glory in the Cross." She had to keep it in her heart and in her mind until the morning. When she awoke, she was able to get to an instrument so that she could sing it and write it on paper.

In "I Will Glory in the Cross," Dottie lays her soul bare before the Lord and refrains from boasting in anything—"good deeds" or any kind "of works," expressing that all glory and praise should "rest upon Him," the One who so willingly died in our place. In the chorus, Dottie says, "I will weep no more for the cross that He bore." Her weeping had turned to glorying in the cross of Christ.

Dottie's song has been recorded by scores of singing groups and has also appeared in songbooks and choral arrangements, much to the delight of singers and congregations everywhere.

Dottie continues, at this time, to travel extensively with her singing ministry.

REFLECTION:
None of us has anything in which to glory, other than the blessed truth of the death, burial, and resurrection of our wonderful Lord. By His marvelous grace He included me—and you—in His family.

23
I Pledge Allegiance to the Lamb

A History-Making Single

I am not ashamed, for I know whom I have believed and am
persuaded that He is able to keep what I have committed to Him
until that Day.

—2 TIMOTHY 1:12

Loving husband, devoted father, former successful businessman, Christian singer and songwriter—all of these describe Ray Boltz, but he is most widely known for his music. One of his most moving and widely used songs is the subject of this story.

Ray is a "Hoosier," born and raised in Muncie, Indiana. As a young boy he had a variety of musical interests, including piano, organ, and woodwind instruments. During his teenage years, Ray, like so many others in that time, became involved in the Woodstock culture, including drugs and alcohol. When he was nineteen, he attended a Christian concert by a group called Fishermen from Anderson University. At that concert Ray committed his life to the Lord.

Even though music was a great part of Ray's life, he graduated from Ball State University with a degree in marketing and became the purchasing director for a manufacturing company. He confessed, "I really enjoy business and had a good career, but music was always in my heart." So in 1986, while his wife, Carol, was pregnant with their fourth child, Ray made the difficult decision to leave his lucrative position and launch out into a full-time concert ministry. Though his first few singing opportunities were in small places with very little financial remuneration, the Lord has since blessed his ministry in ways too numerous to list or mention in this story.

In 1994, Ray's oldest daughter, who was sixteen, was involved with a youth missions group called Teen Mania. She wanted to join them on a mission trip to Africa, but Ray was hesitant about allowing his daughter to travel. After talking with Ron Luce, the leader of the group, Ray and Carol decided to let her go.

Ron asked Ray to write a song for the group to sing in Africa, and so Ray wrote a song titled "I Will Tell the World." Ron then asked if Ray would film a video for the song in Botswana, Africa. He consented to do so and soon found himself on his way to Africa with the group. Part of the video was a drama called "Allegiance" to be performed by the youth group, complete with painted faces, dancing, and mime. The drama asked the question, "Whom is your allegiance to? Is it to God, or is it to someone or something else?"

The audiences in the villages of Botswana eagerly received the teens as they presented their programs. The people realized that the kids were not there for politics, money, or personal gain; they were there to deliver a message. Consequently the African people enthusi-astically received their message.

Ray was deeply moved by the message of the teenagers' drama. He recalls, "On the way home, as we were somewhere over the Atlantic, I began to question my own allegiance. I thought about all of the people who had given their lives for Christ. I asked myself, 'What if I were put in that position? What would my choice be?' I said to myself, 'I hope my allegiance would be to the Lamb.' And so I began to write and continued until the chorus was complete."

Ray enthusiastically woke the youth leader, who was asleep in the seat in front of him, and said, "Ron, Ron, I think God has given me a song based on your drama." Ron groggily nodded his head and went back to sleep. Ray then returned to his song and finished it. When the group returned to America, Ray went into the studio and recorded "I Pledge Allegiance to the Lamb." The next year it won a Dove Award as Inspirational Song of the Year and made music history by topping inspirational music charts as a perfect number one song, receiving 100 points, a first for the *CCM Update* publication.

"I Pledge Allegiance to the Lamb" is a song of commitment to Jesus Christ, the Lamb of God who takes way the sins of the world. It is a pledge of yielding and surrendering to God's will in our lives.

One of Ray's fondest memories of the song is standing on a plat-form in the Mall of America, singing "I Pledge Allegiance to the Lamb," to an audience of 1.3 million men. He was also honored to make a video based on "I Pledge Allegiance to the Lamb." The video storyline is a father teaching his son what becoming a martyr for Christ really means. The record company believed so strongly in the video project that they took Ray to the Coliseum in Rome to record his song for the video. Ray said, "As I found myself standing in the Coliseum, in the place where people had given their lives for their faith in Christ, I was very, very moved."

In the video story a young boy asks his father about martyrs. After the dad carefully explains to his son what it means to be a martyr, he too is taken out and martyred. It is an illustration that challenges people to consider, "What would I do if I were placed in that position?" The video has been viewed around the world, and it reminds Christians of the challenge set before us: Will we pledge our allegiance to our Lord, Jesus Christ?

REFLECTION:

Have you given your whole being—mind, soul, and body—to Jesus Christ? Does He have your complete allegiance? It is not enough just to answer in the affirmative; we must make it so with our very lives.

24
I Worship You, Almighty God

Money Is Involved?

There is none like You, O LORD;
nor are there any works like Your works.

—PSALM 86:8

Sondra Corbett Wood has made a significant contribution to the singing of Christians, especially as they raise their voices in worship to the Lord. She was born in Owenton, Kentucky, and learned to love music as a small child while singing on stage at numerous events with her dad's country band. Early on she learned to play many instruments, including piano, saxophone, and flute.

At age eleven Sondra became a Christian at Sparta Baptist Church in Sparta, Kentucky. She gained musical experience as a teen playing for various school and teen functions in a small band that she and her brother organized. Sondra wrote her first Christian song at age sixteen. Since then she has written more than one hundred songs, with approximately five of them published.

At age eighteen Sondra enrolled in Christ for the Nations Institute in Dallas, Texas. She saw many wonderful praise songs birthed during her time there. She remembers, "When I first arrived at the school, they divided us into groups of four in order for us to get acquainted with other students. Marty Nystrom, author of 'As the Deer,' was part of my group of four. I still consider Marty and his wife, Jeannie, special friends. I also became friends with Tommy Walker, who wrote 'Mourning into Dancing,' and our families still keep in touch. I'm thankful to have had that time in my life."

One Saturday morning, while a student at CFNI, Sondra went to the music building to worship and pray. She was part of a singing group that went out to represent the school, and they were going the following morning to minister at a local church. Sondra wanted to be prepared by praying for the service and for the people who would attend. She also wanted to spend some time in the presence of the Lord, singing to Him. She had no intention of writing a song.

She sat down at a piano in one of the rooms and began to pray and sing. She recalls, "I felt a strong sense of the presence of the Lord. I began to sing, 'I worship You, Almighty God, there is none like You.' When another line came out of my mouth, I thought to myself, 'I'm getting a song here!' I ran out of that little room to the office and asked someone for a pencil and paper, and I quickly jotted down the words and the chords to the song that I had just played and sung."

Sondra explains, "The song came directly from prayer and a desire to commune with the Lord. It was my response. God is the focus of the song. It is a prayer to Him expressing our desire to praise Him and to recognize His righteousness." She gave the song to one of the worship leaders, who taught it to the students at a chapel service. They learned the song very readily and sang it joyfully.

After graduating from CFNI and returning to her small hometown, Sondra's mailbox began to fill up almost on a daily basis with requests to use her song, which had been recorded by Word Music. A friend told Sondra that her song was listed on the cassette tape as "author unknown."

Surprised that her song had been published, Sondra said, "I phoned Word and politely told them that I was the author of the song. The person at Word said to me, "Ma'am, just because you say you wrote a song doesn't mean we are going to send you a check!' I said, 'What do you mean, a check?' I thought to myself, 'Is money involved?' I hadn't thought of that. I was only excited that my song was being used. Shortly after that phone conversation I received my first royalty check in the mail. I was amazed at God."

Not long after that Sondra was contacted by Integrity Music. They wanted to share the rights to her song, and in turn, they would market it on recordings and in songbooks all over the world. That was also very thrilling to Sondra, who never expected the song to be sung across the nation, much less the world. One year later she wrote two verses to the song, and they have been recorded by CFNI on three different occasions.

One of Sondra's fondest memories of the song occurred shortly after it had been taught to the students at the school. Sondra went to one of the buildings where small rooms were set aside for students to go and be alone, to have their quiet times with the Lord. She walked down the hall and opened the door to one of the rooms, not knowing that someone was already using that room. There she saw a young student from Kenya, on his knees with his hands held upward. Tears were streaming down his cheeks, and he was singing, "I Worship You, Almighty God." Sondra slowly closed the door and stepped back into the hallway, her heart welling up within her with joy.

Sondra and her husband, John, have two children and reside in Madison, Wisconsin, where she is the worship leader of Bethesda Christian Fellowship. She also works in the children's ministry, singing and writing songs for the little ones.

SACRIFICE OF PRAISE

REFLECTION:

Worship is a beautiful expression of communion and fellowship with God. When we open our hearts in worship to God, He reveals Himself to us and we are brought closer into His presence. When was the last time you got alone with God and poured out your soul in praise and worship of Him?

25
I Love You, Lord

From a House Trailer by the Highway

We love Him because He first loved us.

—1 JOHN 4:19

In 1950, Oconomowoc, Wisconsin welcomed baby Laurie Brendemuehl. Little did the town realize, of course, that she would grow up to write one of the most popular praise songs of all time. Laurie has loved music since early childhood. Her mom claims that Laurie could sing almost as soon as she could talk. While growing up, Laurie's interest in music intensified and she learned to play a number of instruments, including piano, Autoharp, and guitar. At age sixteen, her first effort at writing songs was a song titled "Loving Unconditionally." This started her on a journey of songwriting that would become a part of her daily quiet times with the Lord.

By age twenty-four, Laurie had met and married Bill Klein, and the Lord had given them their first child, a little girl. Bill was a student at Central Oregon Community College studying Forest Technology; the family was having a difficult time. According to Laurie, they had no extra money, no friends nearby, no church home, and her husband was busy all of the time with his studies. She didn't drive, so she couldn't get away. Her family lived on a highway in a mobile home, so she couldn't even put the baby in a stroller and go for a walk. Their only neighbors were people long retired and tired of life. Laurie vividly remembers those difficult days: "When I needed some encouragement there was no extra money for long-distance calls to family or friends. I was lonely. The only thing I was committed to was trying to get up each morning before our baby, then a toddler, and spend some time with Jesus. I knew that was where the 'life' was."

She would normally get out her Bible and guitar and begin praying and singing songs, trying to find strength to face the day. One day, as she was getting ready for her morning devotional, she realized that she didn't have anything in her to give to Jesus. She knew the right thing to do was to give Him praise, but she just didn't have anything left to offer Him. She recalls, "I was so empty. So I prayed and said to the Lord, 'If You want to hear me sing, would You give me something that You would like to hear?'"

Laurie started strumming on the guitar, and the first two lines of "I Love You, Lord" came out of her mouth with absolutely no effort. She scribbled them on a piece of paper, just in case she would want to remember them and sing them again. She had just come under the teaching of needing to praise God in all things, so those words were very meaningful to her. After she played and sang the beginning of the song again, the last two lines followed just as effortlessly as the first two had come. Describes Laurie, "They just came as a gift from heaven."

"I Love You, Lord" had a great impact on Laurie's life. "Though it is a very simple song, it changed everything for me, and it still is changing life for me. When you are in a dark valley and the Lord gives you light, it makes all the difference, and you keep growing."

Some time later a pastor friend, who was also a musician, came by the Kleins' home to visit and to encourage the struggling young couple. Bill insisted that Laurie sing her song for their friend. He liked "I Love You, Lord" so much that he took it to a national church convention in California and sang it for them. It became the theme song for the convention. As a result, Laurie's song went home with pastors from all over the world, and within a year the Kleins were getting phone calls wondering who owned the song. They hadn't even copyrighted it at that time, since Laurie had no intention of publishing it. "I Love You, Lord" was first recorded by Annie Herring.

Laurie recalls a particularly meaningful experience in the fall of 2000 while she and her husband were in Discipleship Training School at Youth with a Mission in Lakeside, Montana. Late one night in the dormitory, Laurie heard a baby crying somewhere down the hall. She slipped down the hall to the outside of the door just to pray that the baby would be able to sleep. As she was praying outside the door, Laurie heard the mother singing a song to the baby, but the baby kept crying. She then sang "I Love You, Lord" to her child, and while she was singing, the baby fell asleep. The mother had no idea that Laurie was outside the door or that she was the one who had written the song.

Laurie is now a freelance writer of poetry, devotional thoughts, and personal experiences, with some of her poems being published in the secular market. Although she has had approximately a dozen of her songs published, most of them remain in her devotional memoirs.

REFLECTION:
Jesus said that the most important thing for us is to love the Lord our God with all our hearts, all our souls, and with all our minds. These are all interwoven with our worship of Him.

26
Shine, Jesus, Shine

First the UK, Then the World

I am come as a light into the world,
that whoever believes in Me should not abide in darkness.

—JOHN 12:46

In the *Independent on Sunday*, Cole Moreton wrote, "Barely a day goes by without a Kendrick song being sung by a group of Christians somewhere on the planet." Few songwriters from the United Kingdom, or any nation on earth, have touched the lives of God's people as has Graham Kendrick.

Graham, born in 1950 in Northhamptonshire, England, is the son of a Baptist preacher. Although he had prepared himself to be a teacher, he began his singing and songwriting career at age twenty-two. His first efforts in Christian music were contemporary folk music, but he has now moved his skills of storytelling and memorable tunes into a worship vein. As a result, his songs have penetrated deeply into almost every area of Christendom. They aid Christians in the understanding of and participation in the celebration of vital aspects of biblical faith.

Graham is the cofounder of the March for Jesus movement, which had its beginning in the mid-1980s and has involved more than fifty-five million people at prayer, praise, and proclamation events over the years. Graham received a Dove Award in 1995 for his international work. In 2000, Brunei University conferred upon him an honorary doctorate in divinity degree, in recognition of his contributions to the worship life of the church.

Church Copyright License International listings have shown that Graham's songs occupy nine of the spots on their Top 25 list of songs used weekly in a cross-section of United Kingdom churches. His songs are very popular in stadium and other open-air Christian festivals. They have also been used in televised services during times of great national grief. At least two major hymnals have included some of Graham's songs.

When asked the secret of his success, Graham answered, "I don't have any formal musical training and often envy people who do. I've learned mainly by trial and error. I take the 'hit and miss, try it this way, try it that way, hope for happy accidents' approach."

Graham's song "Shine, Jesus, Shine" has become one of the most popular worship songs of the last decade in the United Kingdom. According to Graham, "This song is a prayer for revival. A songwriter can give people words to voice something which is already in their hearts but which they don't have the words or the tune to express, and I think 'Shine, Jesus, Shine' caught a moment when people were beginning to believe once again that an impact could be made on a whole nation."

On his Web site, Graham relates the following story behind the writing of his now-famous song, "Shine, Jesus, Shine":

Bearing in mind the worldwide popularity of this song, perhaps the most surprising thing about the writing of it is the ordinariness of the circumstances. I had been thinking for some time about the holiness of God, and how that as a community of believers and as individuals, His desire is for us to live continually in His presence.

My longing for revival in the Churches and spiritual awakening in the nation was growing, but also a recognition that we cannot stand in God's presence without "clean hands and a pure heart." So I wrote the three verses and "road tested" it in my home church. Though there was clearly merit to the song, it seemed incomplete, so as I was unable at the time to take it any further, I put it back in the file. Several months later I was asked to submit new songs for a conference song book, and as I reviewed this three verse song I realized that it needed a chorus. I remember standing in my music room with my guitar slung around my neck trying different approaches. The line, "Shine, Jesus, Shine" came to mind, and within about half an hour I had finished the chorus, all but some "polishing."

Though I felt an excitement in my spirit at the time, I had no inkling at all that it would become so widely used. There were other songs I rated more highly at the time that most people have never heard of!

Graham and his wife, Jill, have four daughters. The Kendricks attend Ichthus Christian Fellowship, an independent free church, where Graham serves as a member of the leadership team. They make their home in London.

REFLECTION:

The overriding message of "Shine, Jesus, Shine" is that those who follow Christ, the Light of the world, should ask Him to "set our hearts on fire," in a dark world, in order that our "lives tell the story." In that way we point people to the Savior, "the true Light which gives light to every man coming into the world" (John 1:9).

27
As the Deer

On the Nineteenth Day of the Fast

As the deer pants for the water brooks,
so pants my soul for You, O God.

—PSALM 42:1

In 1991, Marty Nystrom entered the Seoul Stadium in Seoul, Korea, and around him were more than one hundred thousand Koreans gathered for a great worship conference. As they opened the conference they began to sing "As the Deer." Marty was deeply moved to think that God had used Him to provide that scriptural song, not only for the people of Korea, but also for Christians around the world.

About his songwriting, Marty shared, "I seem to write songs best when I am not purposefully trying to write one." Such was the case when he wrote the worship song "As the Deer."

Marty was a schoolteacher in Seattle, and since he had the summer off, he decided to go to the summer term of Christ for the Nations Institute in Dallas, Texas. Little did he know what was about to happen to him, especially with all that he would be exposed to and the worship emphasis of the school.

The summer he spent at CFNI was a spiritual renewal time for Marty. He had graduated from Oral Roberts University and, frankly, was a little overwhelmed in ministry. He had been involved in many things at the school, not the least of which was the television ministry of ORU. All of his studies combined with the many other activities had caused stress to take its toll on Marty's spiritual life.

The summer was a time for Marty to restore his passion for Jesus, who had saved him years earlier. He didn't need man's approval or other motivations; it was just time for him to get back to his relationship with Jesus.

Marty's roommate at CFNI was a vibrant Christian who challenged Marty to go on a fast, thinking it would help him to recover his joy. Marty took up the challenge, and on the nineteenth day of the fast, he found himself sitting at a piano in a room of the school, trying to write a song. He was simply playing chord progressions when he noticed a Bible on the music stand of the piano, open to Psalm 42. His eyes fell on the first verse of that chapter. After reading the verse he began to sing its message, right off the page. He wrote the first verse and the chorus of a song, practically straight through. The entire song was completed in a matter of minutes. He then repeated the song he had just written, just to seal it in his mind.

Marty had no intention of showing the song to anyone. It was to be for his own worship time with the Lord. However, before leaving the school to go back to Seattle, he did share it with one person, Dave Butterbaugh, who introduced it to the students at CFN. The song quickly became a favorite.

As was their custom, the school recorded the song and put it into one of their cassette projects that was distributed across the country and to other nations. The next thing Marty knew, "As the Deer" was being sung everywhere. It has now been translated into several different languages and sung in many different styles.

Marty continues to write songs and has authored close to two hundred songs so far in his music ministry career. He also travels the world teaching in worship conferences, spending a considerable amount of time in Asia. He speaks for numerous church retreats for choirs and worship teams in the United States.

Marty and his wife, Jeannie, have been married for twenty years and have two sons, Nathan and Benjamin. They make their home in the Seattle area and attend the Eastside Four Square Church, pastored by Jim Hayford, brother to Jack Hayford, who wrote "Majesty." Marty shares his joy of worship through his many popular albums and CDs.

REFLECTION:

Fortunate is the person who, when thirsty for God, can determine how to remedy the problem, much as Marty did. It can only be done as we find fellowship with the Lord in His Word. Then we rest in Him and praise Him for His goodness.

28
I Want to Be Where You Are

The Violinist Becomes a Logger

He who dwells in the secret place of the Most High
shall abide under the shadow of the Almighty.

—PSALM 91:1

In the late 1960s in Jackson, Mississippi, during a presentation of the opera Carmen, the conductor raised his baton in preparation for his final cutoff. The baton came down and the music ceased. A split second later a young college student in the violin section lowered his instrument. As he did, Don Moen thought, *I've had enough! I quit! I don't know if I want to be a violinist anymore, or even a musician.* And with that he left the concert hall and drove back to the University of Southern Mississippi, picked up his luggage, got into his car with his tuxedo still on, and drove straight through to Minnesota.

A week later he was a lumberjack in the Superior National Forest. He drove a bulldozer, working with a logger who had a long beard, and as he spit, his tobacco juice formed brown icicles at the bottom of his whiskers.

Don recalls, "After a few months of that, sometimes in thirty-below-zero temperatures, sitting on a bulldozer, I thought, 'Maybe playing a violin isn't so bad after all.'" So back to college he went, this time to Oral Roberts University. Don never played the violin seriously again but turned his attention to the guitar and the trombone.

He traveled for a number of years with Terry Law Ministries, after which he spent about three years in Florida writing commercial jingles. He then returned to Tulsa, Oklahoma, and headed up the music division of Terry Law Ministries, which had several groups traveling all over the world.

In 1984, Integrity Incorporated president Michael Coleman approached Moen about serving as worship leader on the seventh Hosanna! Music live praise and worship recording. The resulting project, *Give Thanks,* became one of Integrity's most popular recordings and a benchmark for the genre, achieving gold certification status and selling more than 850,000 copies.

In his current role at Integrity, Moen's impact is felt greatly not only in the company, but also among hundreds of thousands of people worldwide who have been touched by Integrity's music. As Vice President of Creative, Don creates the strategies for the musical direction of numerous high-profile products. In this role, he works closely in the development of worship, choral, and children's products.

Moen also serves as executive producer for many Integrity

releases, working with fellow songwriters and worship leaders and focusing on the research and development of new products. Although deeply involved in product development at Integrity, Moen still takes time for his own creative pursuits. He received Gospel Music Association nominations for his song "God Will Make a Way" and for the album *Worship with Don Moen*. In 1994, he won a Dove Award for the musical *God with Us*.

When reflecting on his many published songs, Don notes that "I Want to Be Where You Are" is one of his favorites. He wrote the song in 1987, while composing the musical *God with Us*. The musical was going to be a journey from the outer court to the inner court of the tabernacle of Moses. Don had studied for about eighteen months on this subject, becoming familiar with the furnishings of the tabernacle, such as the brazen laver, the table of shewbread, and the candlesticks, and how they were symbols of the present time. He also studied about the significance of the holy of holies. In his studies he learned that Christ was revealed in all of these things.

For the opening anthem of the musical he wanted a song that would tell about all of the tribes and tongues coming up to Zion to worship the King. He sat down at the piano to write the anthem and asked himself, *How am I going to write about this journey and make it into a musical?*

Don recalls, "My fingers fell on the keys and I suddenly was playing the musical setting of 'I Want to Be Where You Are,' and the words came with the melody. It just popped out of me. I then thought, 'Now, I have to start over, because the musical cannot start like that. The bridge of the song doesn't even rhyme.' I was simply sketching out things I wanted to say at the time—things that were in my heart. I decided that if I ever wanted to use the song for some other purpose, I would come back and rewrite the lyrics, because they didn't work. I literally threw it aside, thinking, 'This is not the big anthem that I was looking for.'"

Some time later Don was at a church in Oklahoma, visiting the family for whom he had written the song "God Will Make a Way." It was a small church, and they graciously asked Don to sing something. He had brought his legal pad on which he had sketched out the words of "I Want to Be Where You Are," so he sang the song for the small congregation.

Numbers of people came up to Don that day and said, "That is the cry of my heart. I want to be where Christ is." The song deeply impacted people, not because it was well-crafted, but because many people wanted to be where God is, dwelling in His glory. Don states, "I think that is why the song has become so popular: A lot of people identify with it."

Today Don Moen continues to lead thousands of people in worship and praise in many places around the world. He also continues his varied areas of ministry at Integrity Incorporated. Don, his wife, Laura, and their five children make their home in Mobile, Alabama.

REFLECTION:

Many people are hesitant to come into God's presence to worship Him because they feel unworthy. Although we are unworthy in our own flesh, the blood of Jesus Christ has cleansed us and made us new creatures. We can come boldly into His presence, solely because God has ordained it so. We are His children, and He invites us to worship Him.

29
Celebrate Jesus

Launched from a North Texas Kitchen

Why do you seek the living among the dead?
He is not here, but is risen!

—LUKE 24:5–6

Gary Oliver was born in Beaumont, Texas, in 1956. His parents took him to church regularly, and he began singing in church at age three. By age ten he was playing the piano in the church services.

Growing up in a strong Christian household, Gary was always very much aware of God and of his need for a personal relationship with Him. He had a very unusual encounter with the Lord at age ten, when one of his older sisters was diagnosed with a cancerous brain tumor. When he heard the word *cancer* he went to his knees. The instant he knelt down, he felt God's assurance that she was healed. An awesome wave of peace came over Gary's young body, from the top of his head to the soles of his feet. He was assured that God was in control and that his sister would be fine. That was an experience that let him know that God exists and that He is in control.

At age thirteen, in a revival, Gary went to the altar and gave his heart to the Lord, and the Holy Spirit came into his life. Since then the Lord has allowed Gary to do many things, not the least of which is writing more than one thousand songs.

In the early 1980s, Gary became music director of Truth Church in Fort Worth, Texas. During the next several years he wrote and taught the congregation a new chorus each week. As was his custom, on Saturday night he would take his Bible and go to the kitchen, the only room in the house that had space enough for the studio piano. He would read the Bible, pray, and sing from his heart. It was during these Saturday evenings that the Lord would give him a new song to use at church the next day. Gary fondly remembers writing his most popular song, "Celebrate Jesus."

Truth Church was in a particular phase of ministry in which they were trying to do some special things to enhance the children's ministry. One of the ladies who worked with the children's ministry came to him and said, "Pastor Gary, we need to do something for our children so that they will understand the meaning of Easter. We are in a dilemma. We are in a musical for the children, but all of the songs are slow and sad, or they are too complicated for the kids. We want them to know that even though the cross was very sorrowful, there is joy in the resurrection and it is okay to celebrate Easter." Gary agreed, "We need to do something so they can know they can celebrate Him." She said, "That's right." Gary mused aloud, "You know what, that would be a great song!" She replied, "That would be awesome. Would you write the song for us, so that we can teach it to the children?"

So Gary wrote the song with simple words and melody in order for children to understand the reason we celebrate Easter is that Jesus is alive! We serve the only God who died and then rose again from the dead.

Recalls Gary, "I'll never forget the Sunday we sang 'Celebrate Jesus.' As the children of the children's choir were singing the song, the adult choir joined in and the whole place exploded. We sang the song for at least forty-five minutes. It interrupted the whole program." It was then that Gary knew the song was unique.

Some time later, in Stockholm, Sweden, just as Gary walked into the church he was visiting, the congregation started to sing "Celebrate Jesus." Gary was amazed, and he began to weep as he thought how a song written by a young, East Texas boy could go literally around the world and be sung in so many nations. To date, the song has been translated into Russian, Chinese, Japanese, Spanish, French, German, and several African dialects.

Gary Oliver, along with his wife, Toni, pastors a growing church, the Tabernacle of Praise in Forth Worth, Texas.

REFLECTION:

Gary has reminded us of the valuable and soul-stirring truth that Christianity is only way of life that is sustained by a risen Lord!

30
I Want to Do Thy Will, O Lord

Not Above Average

*For whoever does the will of God is My brother
and My sister and mother.*

—MARK 3:35

The music ministry of the Goss Brothers was abruptly ended with the untimely death of older brother James Goss in a plane crash. This was tragic news to many gospel music lovers, and especially to Goss Brothers fan clubs that were springing up in various cities. The influence of their short tenure as a singing group is still felt today among many Christian singers and songwriters. One of their most popular songs, "I Want to Do Thy Will, O Lord," was written by Roni Goss and deals with the specific will of God in the life of a Christian.

Roni Goss, born in Cartersville, Georgia, has made significant contributions to the singing of Christians in the United States and abroad. He had the happy privilege of being born into a family of Christian musicians. He was the middle son of a trio of boys that would help make the Goss name synonymous with beautiful Christian music—music of great variety and purpose.

As a small lad Roni sang with his brothers, James and Lari, in Center Baptist Church, a church that his grandfather founded and where his dad led the congregational singing and his mom played the piano. All three of the young Goss brothers learned to play the piano and to sing together with beautiful harmonies. Churches welcomed them, as did the radio station WBHF in Cartersville.

When Roni was eighteen, he and his siblings formed the Goss Brothers, a traveling singing group. Stylistically and in content they were far ahead of their time, but in one area they came up a little short, according to Roni, who said, "We were not above average vocally." All three brothers had mid-range voices. They overcame the fact that none of them sang very high or very low by arranging unusually close harmonies.

In those days, members of singing groups invited to perform at concert halls often gathered around the Goss Brothers backstage to listen to their unique arrangements. Roni said, "We often sold more records backstage than out front." The musicians and singers had a much better appreciation for the Goss Brothers than the people in the seats who had come to hear the sounds of southern gospel music.

After the plane accident that took the life of his brother James, Roni went on to other musical interests, including studio singing and piano and keyboard accompaniment. He regularly plays keyboard for the international television programs *Unfolding Majesty, Music That Ministers,* and *Love Special,* all seen around the world on TBN.

One day in the mid-1960s, Roni was in conversation with H. P. Vibbert, a pastor and good friend, concerning the will of God in the lives of Christians. Vibbert had recently preached a sermon in which he spoke of God taking us, breaking us, molding us, and making us for the express purpose of doing His will. Vibbert stressed the fact that sometimes God chooses to make His children willing to do His will by sending what appear to be adversities along life's pathway. Roni told his friend, "That would make a good song." So he took Vippert's thoughts and molded them into a lyric. He then wrote a musical setting and titled the song "I Want to Do Thy Will, O Lord."

Soon afterward the Oak Ridge Boys, good friends of Roni, asked if he had any songs that he could suggest for a new project they were about to record. He replied, "Yes, I have a few songs." So he played and sang for them several songs that he had written, one of which was "I Want to Do Thy Will, O Lord." The Oak Ridge Boys chose to record two of the songs, one being "I Want to Do Thy Will, O Lord," launching it on its way into the hearts and lives of multitudes of Christians. It was later published, making it easier for worship leaders to lead congregations in this musical prayer of consecration.

The lyrics' prayer to God asking Him to take, break, mold, and make us, is difficult for any Christian to sing and really mean it. "I Want to Do Thy Will, O Lord," which is also the first line of the song, has made its way into thousands of churches and youth groups across America, and it has become one of the great songs of commitment used by pastors, youth workers, and evangelists.

Roni and his wife, Linda, live near Atlanta, Georgia. They have one son, Nathan, who is the singles' pastor of a church in Gainesville, Georgia. Roni's brother Lari is an enormously talented and popular songwriter, producer, arranger, and keyboardist.

REFLECTION:

The most important thing in the life of a Christian is to do the will of God. Our example in this essential relationship with our Lord is Christ Himself, who lived totally and completely in the will of His heavenly Father (see John 4:34).

31
People Need the Lord

A Waitress Inspires a Song

For God did not send His Son into the world to condemn the world,
but that the world through Him might be saved.

—JOHN 3:17

He is a songwriter who has that certain something that you can't put your hand on—a gift from God. Wishing and hoping for his ability is fruitless. You can hone it, but you can't own it completely, apart from God's endowment. He looks out of a different window." That is Greg Nelson's assessment of master poet Phill McHugh, with whom he has cowritten many songs.

Both Greg and Phill grew up in the Midwest: Greg is from Bismarck, North Dakota, and Phill from Aberdeen, South Dakota. As a team they have written scores of praise and worship songs, some of which have already become standards that will likely be sung by Christians around the world until the Lord returns. They first met in Greg's recording studio in North Dakota. Several years later they moved to Nashville, became reacquainted, and started cowriting songs.

Greg was born into a musical family—his mother was a pianist, and his father was a singer. In addition to their church music, they produced and directed operas and operettas. Greg learned piano and music theory from his mother. He, his sister, Sigrid, and his brother, Corliss, played classical music as a trio while still children: Greg on cello, Sigrid on piano, and Corliss on violin. By age twenty-one Greg was conductor of the Bismarck Civic Orchestra, a position that he maintained for several years.

Phill had very little formal music training outside of a few piano lessons. Yet he has loved music since his early years, with a great appreciation for all kinds and styles. As a college-age young man, he became involved with the culture of the late 1960s, traveling and performing in clubs of various kinds. Phill says, "All of this affected me a great deal and drove me to look for answers. I began to read the Bible on my own, which started a process that led to my conversion."

Greg and Phill, separately and as cowriters, have been instrumental in writing hundreds of songs, with many of them published. Their creations have been recognized with numerous awards.

One day, Greg and Phill were trying to write a song and spent most of the morning talking about ideas. They decided, about lunchtime, to go to a nearby restaurant. After they were seated, a waitress came to their table, and as she approached them she smiled. Yet to Greg and Phill it seemed that her eyes were so empty. She was trying to convey a cheery attitude, but her face seemed to say something else. She took their order and walked away.

They looked at each other and said, "She needs the Lord." Greg and Phill then began looking around the restaurant at all of the people. They too seemed to have emptiness in their faces. The two men sensed a real heaviness in their hearts as they watched the other customers.

They recall about the experience, "Suddenly we realized that all of those people need the Lord. Just as quickly, we both thought, 'We need to write that—people need the Lord.' We finished our meal and went back to the office and sat down to write what was in our hearts. The pictures from the restaurant that remained in our minds, coupled with the realization that millions of people around the world are also groping for some ray of light, gave rise to 'People Need the Lord.'"

God has his own timing and orchestrates all things under His control. Consequently, it was three years before the song was recorded. Greg and Phill had tried to interest several recording artists in the song, but they just didn't "get it." Finally, the song was presented to Steve Green. He immediately sensed the importance of the song's message and was excited to sing it.

With the faces of the "empty people" in the restaurant still in their minds, Greg and Phill, in the first verse, described the plight of those who go through "private pain," and from "fear to fear," going "who knows where." In the second verse, they declare to you and me the awesome responsibility of taking the message of Christ to a lost and dying world, "sharing life with one who's lost." Only through Christ's love can people's pain be transferred to our hearts. The chorus reminds us, not once, but five times, that "people need the Lord."

"People Need the Lord" is the most often used of all of Greg and Phill's songs. Greg remembers, to his great joy and delight, that he has heard it in a number of different languages in other countries. It was also used in the Billy Graham crusades in Europe, which to him was very heartwarming. Of all the songs that he has had part in writing, Greg expressed that "People Need the Lord" is one of his favorites.

The element that makes the song so meaningful, to almost every Christian who hears it, is the compelling melody that carries its lyrics, driving the heart cry of lost humanity right into our very souls.

REFLECTION:

You and I don't have to go to a foreign land to find people who are without Christ. We need only to go across the aisle at work, at school, at the office, or across the driveway to the house next door. All around us, people need the Lord.

32
All Hail King Jesus

Surprised by a Song

Keep this commandment without spot, blameless until our Lord Jesus Christ's appearing, which He will manifest in His own time, He who is the blessed and only Potentate, the King of kings and Lord of Lords.

—1 TIMOTHY 6:14–15

To have your very first published song travel around the world and be sung in many languages is a blessing that defies description. That is exactly what happened in the life of Dave Moody after he wrote his majestic worship song "All Hail King Jesus."

He experienced that joy firsthand when he visited churches in India and Japan in 1987, only ten years after writing the song. He says, "I had no idea that people over there even knew the song, so to have heard it sung in those nations, not expecting anything of that nature, was probably the most significant feeling I've ever experienced regarding my song."

Dave became a Christian at a very early age during an altar call in his church in Vancouver, British Columbia. His parents saw to it that Dan had every opportunity to further his music goals. They started him on accordion lessons at age ten and then piano at age twelve. Through his teen years he worked hard toward a goal of being a piano teacher.

As he grew into his teen years, his brother, Doug, music director of Fairwood Assembly of God Church in the Seattle, Washington area, took him under his wing and began to mentor him and to teach him how to arrange music for choirs, quartets, trios, and other groups in the church. He even taught Dave to direct the choir in his absence. Both brothers directed the hundred-voice choir from the piano. In 1970, Dave graduated from the Royal Conservatory of Music in Toronto with a piano teaching degree. He then taught piano for fourteen years. Four years after his graduation, he wrote his first song during a children's camp. Since then he has written approximately thirty songs and praise choruses.

He wrote his now famous song, "All Hail King Jesus," in 1977 while preparing to teach some piano lessons. The youngsters were to come for their lessons after school, beginning about 3:30 P.M. On that particular afternoon Dave had some time before they arrived, so he sat down at the piano and began worshiping the Lord.

"The farthest thing from my mind was writing a song," admitted Dave. "My only purpose was to spend time with the Lord. Quite suddenly, I began to develop a melody that was coming to me— something I had never played before. And just as quickly came some words that I began to sing, using the melody the Lord was giving.

When I finished, I realized that the Lord had given me a song. I played it over several times and put it on paper so I wouldn't forget it. During the next couple of days I played it for a couple of friends, Gil and Sue, just to see their response, which was very favorable."

The following Sunday Dave was anxious to share "All Hail King Jesus" with the congregation. He happened to be directing the music that day in the absence of his brother, Doug. From his position at the organ, he sang the song a couple of times, allowing the congregation to learn it. He then asked them to sing it through with him. They did so and afterward sat with very passive and stoic expressions. Dave thought the song had flopped. Then he said to himself, *Well, maybe they just don't know it well enough.* So he sang it through again with them. As the congregation was finishing the song, the associate pastor, Lou Peterson, leading the service in the absence of the pastor, stepped over to Dave and asked that he sing it with them again, and Dave did so. He recalls, "As we were nearing the end of the song I opened my eyes, and to my surprise I saw the congregation of more than eight hundred people on their knees, with their hands raised toward heaven, singing my song." It was an experience long to be remembered by Dave and the entire congregation.

As people sing Dave's song everywhere, and as the different names given to the Lord Jesus, such as "Morning Star," "King of kings," and "Lord of lords," flow from the congregation, it creates a wonderful spirit of joy and worship. "All Hail King Jesus" has been placed in a number of hymnals and has been arranged into choral settings, greatly helping it to be sung and heard by thousands of people worldwide. It has also been recorded by scores of recording artists and choral groups.

Dave is now on the pastoral staff of Fairwood Church and has continued to write songs, although none so well known as "All Hail King Jesus." Dave and his wife, Karen, have two grown children who are also faithfully serving the Lord.

REFLECTION:

There is something about the names of Jesus that evokes a spirit of worship in all of us who know him as personal Savior and Lord. Praise Him today as the King of your life.

33
I Exalt Thee

I Stepped into "Another Room"

For You, LORD, are most high above all the earth;
You are exalted far above all gods.

—PSALM 97:9

Martin Luther, the man who launched the Protestant Reformation, once said, "Next to the Word of God, music deserves the highest praise. The gift of language combined with the gift of song was given to man that he should proclaim the Word of God through music. We must teach music in the schools; a schoolmaster ought to have skill in music or I would not regard him; neither should we ordain men as preachers unless they have been exercised in music."

We would not all agree with Luther's opinion, but Christ Covenant Church in Houston, Texas, is blessed to have such a pastor in Pete Sanchez, Jr. His degree in music, his piano ability, and his songwriting all contribute to the praise and worship program, as well as every other area of the music ministry in his church. As a musically gifted pastor, he is better able to understand the needs and the work of the musicians under his ministry.

Pastor Sanchez was born in Houston as one of eight children, and music became important to Sanchez early in life. He grew up in a broken and disadvantaged home, so the church became a refuge for him. A kind church organist took Pete under her wing and encouraged him. He began to play the piano at about age seventeen.

One of Pete's best-known songs is "I Exalt Thee," which he penned almost three decades ago. "I love to write from the Psalms," Pete shares. "One of my goals as a songwriter is to have written a song from each of the 150 Psalms in my lifetime. In my private devotional periods I spend a lot of time in that book of the Bible." It was during one of those quiet times with the Lord that Pete came across Psalm 97:9: "For You, Lord are most high above all the earth; You are exalted far above all gods." Pete wrote a tune so that he could sing those words.

During his quiet sessions with the Lord in those days, Pete would often sit at the piano and sing the first half of what is now the song, "I Exalt Thee." Each time he worshiped God in that manner, the song would come out. Although he sometimes sensed that something was lacking at the end of the song, he didn't know just what, so he decided to be content with what the Lord had already given him. After all, he was the only one hearing or singing it.

The following year, sometime in the spring, Pete was waiting one Sunday morning for his wife to finish getting dressed for church. As was his habit, he sat down at the piano and began to sing, "For Thou, O Lord, art high . . ." This time, as he got to the end of his song, Pete says, "I stepped into 'another room.' A new chorus for the song came as I was sitting there. I knew as I began to sing it that something special was taking place in my life. It was a very powerful moment."

When he finished the song, Pete thought, *Well, something just happened, but I don't know just what.* He still assumed that the song was only for his private times with the Lord, so he didn't mention it to anyone else. Pete and Karen went on to the New Testament Baptist Church in Houston that morning. As things happen that are orchestrated by God, when they reached the church Pete was asked to present some special music, so he sang "I Exalt Thee." It had a profound effect on the congregation, which really surprised Pete.

He didn't sing it again until a few weeks later when he was asked to attend a songwriters' conference in Mississippi. Each of the songwriters was asked to present three songs. Pete was the last person to present a song. He presented two of his "well-written" compositions and received only polite applause and mild appreciation.

Then Pete was asked, "Do you have another song to present?" The only fresh thing he had was "I Exalt Thee." He began to sing his new song, much like the two previous songs, with no visible response. But when he came to the chorus, the effect was almost immediate. People stood to their feet and sang with their full voices, many of them with their hands in the air.

Pete recalls, "I watched this explosion of worship that was totally unexpected or anticipated. I was the most shocked of all the people in the room. To me it was only a little song that the Lord had given to me for my quiet times, but here was God touching lives with my simple song. I had never intended to share it except, perhaps, on some special occasion."

Pete copyrighted "I Exalt Thee" and put it into a collection of songs that he had written, but he never tried to promote it. In 1983, Phil Driscoll picked it up and used it in his album *I Exalt Thee,* which was nominated for a couple of awards. Pete then began to be flooded with mail from every major publisher in the United States and from many other countries. He later was asked to do a project with Integrity Music, on which the song was included, getting the song out to a wider audience.

One of the greatest blessings concerning the song that God gave to Pete was when he heard a tape recording of a Francis Schaffer conference overseas. People were singing "I Exalt Thee" in ten different languages, all at the same time.

Pete Sanchez, Jr., is the senior pastor of Christ Covenant Church in Houston, Texas. He is also a vital part of Integrity Incorporated, presently serving as Educational Program Coordinator for Integrity Worship Ministries, a training institute for worship leaders and songwriters. He estimates that he has written approximately two hundred songs.

Pastor Sanchez and his wife, Karen, have two children, Elita and Scott. They would be thrilled if you joined them in one of their services at Christ Covenant Church when your travels take you to the Houston area.

REFLECTION:

When we come into the presence of the Lord to praise and exalt Him, He brings joy and strength into our lives. He tells us in Psalm 16:11, "In Your presence is fullness of joy," and in Nehemiah 8:10, "The joy of the LORD is your strength."

34
Oh How He Loves You and Me

Not Enough Original Lyric

*In this is love, not that we loved God, but that He loved us and
sent His Son to be the propitiation for our sins.*

—1 JOHN 4:10

Kurt Kaiser is one of the greatest musicians that Christianity has
ever known. For more than forty years his name has been
synonymous with Christian keyboard artistry, songwriting,
conducting, and arranging. In 1992, Kurt was awarded a special
Lifetime Achievement Award by the American Society of
Composers, Authors, and Publishers for his contribution to the
Christian music industry. His piano album *Psalms, Hymns, and
Spiritual Songs* won a Dove Award.

Kurt was born in the "windy city," Chicago, Illinois, in 1934. He
recalls, "I was seven years old when one Sunday evening we were all
gathered around the piano in the living room of our home, singing,
as was our custom each week. I began having a real urge from the
Spirit of God to know Him and to give my heart and life to Christ.

135

My mother went with me to my bedroom, we knelt down by the bed, and I accepted Christ into my life." Kurt's family attended a Plymouth Brethren church that was simply called the Assembly That Meets on Barry Avenue. Although they allowed no keyboard instruments of any kind in the church, Kurt had outlets for his Christian music in other places, such as the radio ministry of Moody Bible Institute in Chicago.

From the young age of four Kurt had private piano teachers. This continued throughout his high school years and on through college. In Lane Technical High School, he majored in piano as well as played cello in the school orchestra. After high school he studied at the American Conservatory of Music in Chicago. He then enrolled in Northwestern University, where he earned two degrees.

In 1959, he joined Word Incorporated as Director of Artists and Repertoire, and he later became Vice President and Director of Music. It was not until 1969 that he had the opportunity to try his hand at songwriting. He and Ralph Carmichael cowrote a musical, *Tell It Like It Is,* out of which came Kurt's very popular song "Pass It On." Since then he began to write very seriously and has now written more than four hundred songs.

"Through the years I have been in the habit of keeping my ears tuned to things that people say, a phrase that may give me an idea for a song. I'll write it down quickly. I may come across a musical refrain or a lyrical idea that I can file away in a special place in my office.

Occasionally I will pull these things out and look at them. One day I came across this line, "Oh how He loves you and me," and I wrote it down. I remember very well writing it across the top of a piece of manuscript paper, and that's all I had. I then sat down to think about that phrase and the whole song quickly came to me. I could not have spent more than ten or fifteen minutes writing the whole of it. That's how rapidly it all came, the lyrics and the melody together. I sent it off to secure a copyright.

"I could not believe what came back in the mail. The Copyright Office in Washington said that there was not enough original lyric to warrant granting a copyright. I was extremely disappointed because I knew the song was very singable. A couple of days went by and I decided to write a companion verse, or a second set of lyrics. I sent it back to Washington and this time I got the copyright."

"Oh How He Loves You and Me" has traveled far and wide and into the hearts of millions of people. Many hymnals and chorus books have included it, as well as numerous choral collections. There is no telling how many times it has been recorded since it was written in 1975. The message of Christ's journey to Calvary, showing just how much He loves you and me, is truly soul-stirring.

The Lord has singularly blessed the ministry of Kurt Kaiser. He has recorded sixteen solo albums at the piano and has arranged and produced albums for many gifted artists, including Diane Bish, Ernie Ford, Larnelle Harris, Jerome Hines, Burl Ives, George

REFLECTION:

The strongest drive that manifests itself within every human being is the need to be loved by someone. Only when we get to heaven will we be able to understand God's love for us—the real meaning of the cross of Jesus Christ.

35
You Are My All in All

Playing Only with His Left Hand

I can do all things through Christ who strengthens me.

—PHILIPPIANS 4:13

If we were to ask Dennis Jernigan to start listing the blessings of God in his life on this earth, he would assure us that they are too numerous to count. But should he attempt such a list, it would certainly start out like this: Melinda, Israel, Anne, Hannah, Glory, Judah, Galen, Raina, Ezra, and Asa, his wife and their nine wonderful children. Those are the people that he is able to draw around him and love as they love him.

Dennis was born in 1979, in Sapulpa, Oklahoma. During Dennis's early years, his father led the singing in the First Baptist Church of Boynton, Oklahoma, and continues to do so to this day. Playing the piano came very easily for Dennis, and by age nine he was regularly playing for the worship services at the church. He learned to play by ear and as a child spent hours practicing at his grandmother Jernigan's house. She taught him how to play chords on the piano and was a great spiritual influence in his life.

Dennis enrolled in Oklahoma Baptist University and later said of the experience: "Because of my lack of musical studies growing up, my training at OBU was like learning a whole new language. To be able to actually read and write the music I could see and hear opened up a whole new world. That ability would be very valuable later in life as I started to express my heart and feelings in song."

Several years ago, Dennis led a weekday morning prayer group in Oklahoma City in early worship and prayer. He would sit at the piano and lead in certain aspects of worship as the people had particular needs brought to their minds.

One morning in 1989, he was focusing on interceding for other people in general and remembering what the Lord had done for him, particularly. As he thought on those things, a melody began to form in his mind and he played it on the piano. Lyrics came at the same time, and Dennis began to sing, "You are my strength when I am weak . . ." and so on. The lyrics came so quickly for Dennis that he continued playing the new melody only with his left hand while he put the song on manuscript paper with his right hand. He continued until he had written the complete song, just as it exists today.

"The next morning I sang it with the prayer group," Dennis says. "They picked it up quickly and began to enthusiastically sing it with me. The whole of the song is a prayer set to music. We used it for about a year before I recorded it. By way of that recording and by word of mouth it began to be known far and wide."

Word Music recorded the song about two years later. From there it has been carried to many other places in the world and has been placed in chorus books, choir arrangements, and hymnals, thus making it widely accessible to the general population.

The chorus is a tribute to Jesus as the Lamb of God, whose name is worthy of our praise. The verses are recognitions of our weaknesses and need and His ability to supply and give victory in our lives. To date, Dennis has written between two and three thousand songs, with about 250 of them recorded or published.

Dennis and his family call Boynton home, but they actually live some sixteen miles away near Muskogee, Oklahoma. A sign at the Boynton city limits announces: "Home of Dennis Jernigan: Christian Songwriter and Author." The Jernigan's are founding members of New Community Church, where Dennis leads worship about twice each month. He also pastors a small home group as part of the church.

REFLECTION:

Before the Lord can help us, we must recognize our flaws and our daily need for His providential care and supply. As our own private worship should be, this song is a declaration of yielding to Jesus as the Lamb of God in the midst of our failures and fears.

36
How Excellent Is Thy Name

Finally, Some Lyrics for My Music

O LORD our Lord, how excellent is Your name in all the earth!

—PSALM 8:9

There are very few husband-and-wife teams writing praise and worship songs, one of which is Dick and Melodie "Mel" Tunney. The Tunneys have a wide variety of musical interests in ministry as duet performers, solo artists, producers, arrangers, composers, and studio musicians. The Tunneys have received several awards, and they have made a major impact on the genre of contemporary worship music.

Mel was born in Fort Worth, Texas, in 1960, into a very musical home. Her dad was a minister of music and a songwriter, with one song published in the *Baptist Hymnal*. Her mom was a church organist and pianist. Mel took piano lessons and sang in church choirs and ensembles. Although she sang her first solo at age three, she began to sing seriously at age twelve.

Dick, born in Dayton, Ohio, in 1956, wanted to play trumpet at age five, so his parents took him to a music store where they found out that he couldn't play trumpet without front teeth. They bought him an accordion instead, and at age seven he won a national accordion competition. He began playing piano at age nine, and through junior and senior high school played in school bands. He attended Cumberland College in Williamsburg, Kentucky, where he was student band director his last three years.

Dick and Mel met while singing in Truth, a touring Christian music ensemble. During those days Mel began to seriously try her hand at songwriting and was encouraged to have at least one of her songs recorded by Truth. One day while at a particular church, Dick came upon Mel in one of the church classrooms, sitting at a piano, laboring over a composition she had started. Dick offered some suggestions, and thus began a very successful songwriting duo, with presently more than 150 songs to their credit, many of which are widely known. They continued traveling together with Truth for about eighteen months.

In 1981, one year after he and Mel had married, Dick was on the road playing for the Imperials, a southern gospel quartet. The lead singer in the quartet, Paul Smith, was a lyricist of some talent, and they repeatedly said to each other, "We should write something together." But they just never got around to it.

Paul's mother and father-in-law had a cabin on a lake not too far from the Tunneys' home, and he invited Dick and Mel to come to the cabin for a fish fry to be held several days from that time. The Tunneys gladly accepted the invitation. Upon arriving back in town from a visit with friends, they drove straight out to the cabin, situated on a lake.

As Dick and Mel were leaving the fish fry, Paul said, "Wait a minute. I have some lyrics that I want to give you." He had a verse about half-finished, with a chorus that was taken from Psalm 8:9. During the thirty minutes it took them to drive home, Mel considered a melody that would be suitable for Paul's lyrics, and then she exclaimed, "I've got it!" Several weeks earlier, Mel had composed a melody that she had no lyrics for, not even an idea. She realized that Paul's lyrics were a perfect fit to her music. After they reached their home, Dick and Mel finished the project in about two hours. They completed the lyrics for the verses and put the music with it.

Mel explained, "The musical setting came first and then the lyrics fit it perfectly. Usually we pretty much get the lyrics and the melodies at the same time, but this time it was different. I wrote the music and then said to myself, 'I don't have any clue what is going to happen to this.'" They were delighted that they finally had lyrics that would fit with the musical setting.

Dick added, "When we showed the song to Greg Nelson, he said, 'If you increase the length of the chorus, I think Larnelle Harris will cut it.'" Mel quickly agreed. Larnelle Harris did record the song, and it won a Dove Award for Song of the Year in 1987. Dick continued, "At that time we were very praise-oriented in our song-writing. God was really blessing what we were doing, and it was a wonderful period in our lives."

Dick and Melodie continue to travel, presenting their music, and are busy with myriad other projects. The Tunneys and their two daughters, Whitney Lane and Kelsey Shea, are members of Christ Community Church in Franklin, Tennessee. They reside in Brentwood, Tennessee.

REFLECTION:

The name of the Lord our God excels them all. His name alone is worthy of our praise. We should say with the psalmist, "Let them praise the name of the Lord: for His name alone is excellent: His glory is above the earth and heaven" (Psalm 148:13).

37
I Sing Praises

To Sing It or Not to Sing It

Sing to the LORD, bless His name.... For the LORD is
great and greatly to be praised.

—PSALM 96:2, 4

Terry MacAlmon has made a real impact on the downtown area of Colorado Springs, Colorado. Every Wednesday, during the noon hour, between three hundred and four hundred people meet with him at the World Prayer Center for a season of praise and worship. There is no preaching and no teaching other than the songs being led by Terry. Between forty and fifty different churches are represented from many different denominations.

Terry was born in Poughkeepsie, New York, and was considered by some to be a child prodigy. He began playing the piano at age three and continued to develop on his own until age eight, when his parents coaxed him to take piano lessons. Of his piano lessons Terry says, "That was a disaster that lasted for about two months." By age eleven he was the church pianist for First Assembly of God Church in Lexington, Kentucky.

Terry later became a student at the University of Kentucky, where he studied voice. In addition to his piano, he played trumpet for a number of years. At the age of eighteen, he began to write songs under the inspiration of the Lord. To date, Terry has written approximately 150 songs, with around thirty of them being recorded or published.

Terry's story concerning the writing of "I Sing Praises" is most unusual. In 1986, he was serving as a worship pastor at Resurrection Fellowship in Loveland, Colorado. As was their custom, the ministry leaders of the church would meet for prayer thirty minutes before each service. One Sunday evening, during one of their prayer times, Terry was quietly worshiping the Lord when suddenly the Lord gave him a song. Says Terry, "It was as if the Lord went over to the music library of heaven and took something out of the 'I' file and dropped it right into my heart." He began to quietly sing, "I sing praises to Your name, O Lord . . ." Realizing that the Lord was giving him a new melody and new lyrics, Terry took a piece of paper from his Bible and jotted down the words and a rough melody line as the song was being given to him. He then placed the paper back into his Bible.

Later that evening Terry was sitting at the piano leading the music portion of the service. When he came to a transition period, where he usually went from more upbeat melodies to slower worship songs, Terry sensed the Holy Spirit saying to him, "Teach the new song." Terry silently protested, *THAT song? There's nothing to that song. It has no substance, and it's too simple.* Terry sat and stared at the keys for what seemed like an eternity, trying to decide: to sing it, or not to sing it. About two thousand people were awaiting his decision.

Finally, Terry went with the more positive urge and said, "Folks, I would like to teach you a song that the Lord gave to me just before the service tonight." He began to sing "I Sing Praises." He was amazed at the response of the congregation. "Immediately I sensed victory in my heart, because the people began to sing with me almost before I had sung through it the first time. We sang it again and again. God used His song and my less-than-immediate obedience to bless His children with the music of heaven."

Terry had a small band behind him, and the bass player, Neal Marchman, stepped up to him after the service and said, "Pastor Terry, when you taught 'I Sing Praises' tonight, the Lord showed me that song being sung in nations all over the world." Terry just smiled and said, "Neal, thank you, but you're crazy!" Two years later, Terry submitted the song to Integrity Music. They liked it so much that they included it on an album titled *Enter His Gates.*

Today "I Sing Praises" rates very high in the Top 50 songs of Integrity Music. Terry receives reports that it is also being sung in many other countries, including England, Canada, Mexico, China, Russia, Argentina, and the Philippines. Its popularity is still on the rise more than a decade since it first was recorded. The song can be found in hymnals, chorus books, and some of the newest collections of praise and worship choral music, in addition to having been recorded by other music companies.

Terry and his wife, Greta, have three sons, and make their home in Colorado Springs, Colorado. He continues to travel around the United States, leading praise and worship.

REFLECTION:

Terry's song reminds us that our Lord is great, and He is greatly to be praised. God's invitation to come before Him with thanksgiving and praise is not confined to church services alone. We can praise His name anywhere we can commune with Him.

38
Lord, Be Glorified

A Song Only for the Three of Us

I will praise You, O LORD my God, with all my heart,
and I will glorify Your name forevermore.

—PSALM 86:12

He has performed under the watchful eye of Polish KGB agents, at Hyde Park in London, to a planeload of passengers at thirty-seven thousand feet, in the bustees of Calcutta, in the slums of Mexico City, in the subways of Germany, on the campuses of South Africa, and, at his mother's request, to the people in a California fruit stand. Add to this several thousands of appearances in churches, youth conventions, music festivals, television programs, in addition to writing many favorite worship songs, and you have an idea of the music ministry of Bob Kilpatrick.

This Louisville, Kentucky, native was the middle of five children born to the family of a Southern Baptist air force chaplain. His mom declared that young Bob was singing by age two and could harmonize with others on such songs as "Ain't Gonna Study War No

More." Bob remembers happy times in the car when the family would pick out things to sing about as they drove along. His music interest continued into high school, where he played in the orchestra.

Chaplain Kilpatrick's travels landed the family in Istanbul, Turkey. During his tenure there, the Kilpatrick children attended a school four hundred miles from Istanbul. While out from under his parents' supervision, young Bob began to make some poor choices. Consequently, his parents thought it necessary to send him back to the United States to live with his cousins in Georgia.

While in Georgia, a friend took Bob on a retreat where he was drawn to Jesus and felt strongly that he needed Him. He stood up in a meeting and committed himself to Christ. When Bob was eighteen, he moved with his family to California, where he had an overwhelming experience of total commitment of his heart to the Lord.

Concerning the writing of his songs, Bob says, "When I became committed to Jesus, we went to the streets trying to tell people about Christ, all up and down California. I seemed to continually have an acoustic guitar in my hands, so it came natural to make up songs to sing for the people who would listen. After a while I realized, 'Maybe I have a talent for this. Maybe I should give the rest of my life to it.'"

Since that time Bob has written approximately four hundred

songs, with approximately 175 of them being recorded or published by major Christian music companies. He admits, "After the Lord gives me a song, I play it for my wife, Cindy. I want to please the Lord first, then Cindy."

In 1977, at age twenty-four, Bob was alone in his mother-in-law's living room in Atwater, California. He had his Bible open on his knees and his guitar in his hands. Before he began writing, he paused and prayed, "Lord, I'd like to write a song, and I don't want others to sing it. I want it to be a private prayer of dedication for Cindy and me to sing before our concerts." At that time Cindy was traveling and singing with Bob. He then said, "Lord, I'd like the song to be only for the three of us."

Bob then began to put the song together. Cindy came into the room and asked, "What are you up to?" Bob replied, "I'm writing a song, but I'm having a little trouble with a certain part of it." He sang it for her, and Cindy made a helpful suggestion. She then suggested, "You should sing that tomorrow morning at church." Bob was planning to attend the chapel service of the Castle Air Force Base with Cindy's family, and he had been invited to sing there. Despite Bob's intentions to keep the song to himself, the next day he sang it for the small congregation.

A week later Bob met up with Karen Lafferty, who was leaving almost immediately for a tour in Europe, and he shared the song with her and her keyboard player. She took the song to Europe, and the keyboard player, who didn't make that trip, took it to Calvary Chapel in Costa Mesa, California, where the congregation sang "Lord, Be Glorified" every Saturday night for the next two years.

Bob says, "Not long after that, I was touring the Maranatha Music complex and met Tommy Coomes, head of Artist and Repertoire, in the hallway. He said, 'We would like to record your song, but we need to change the girls' part,' referring to the obbligato-like part that Cindy had suggested. I said, 'No, I really like the girls' part.' He said, 'Then we probably won't use it.' I went outside and began to kick myself, because everything I wanted to happen was happening, and I was too stubborn to change my song."

Four months went by, and then Coomes called Bob. He said, "We just finished recording your song, and I need to get a license for it." Bob asked, "Is Maranatha going to publish it?" Coomes replied, "No, you are."

Little did Tommy Coomes know what a gift he was giving to Bob and Cindy. The royalties from that one song helped finance their ministry to churches. Maranatha recorded "Lord, Be Glorified" fifty times in the following two years. Other major companies began to record and publish it. It was placed in chorus books, hymnals, and choral arrangements with an inestimable number of copies being printed.

Bob recalls, "Years later, as I was having lunch with Tommy Coomes, I thanked him for allowing me to keep the copyright to my song and for not requiring that Maranatha publish it after they recorded it. He said, 'I don't know why I didn't publish your song. I had never failed to do that before, nor have I failed to do it since.'"

Bob Kilpatrick knows that God orchestrates the affairs in the lives of His children—those who want to please Him in everything. Bob and Cindy live in Fair Oaks, California, where Bob is president and founder of Bob Kilpatrick Ministries and a new music label, Fair Oaks Music. Bob continues with a heavy schedule of traveling, song-writing, and sponsoring young musicians starting their music ministries. In 1999, he was the third inductee into the Assemblies of God Music Hall of Honor.

REFLECTION:

It is wonderful to sing songs of praise and worship to our heavenly Father, and yet, as Bob's song suggests, He should "be glorified" in our very lives—mere words are not enough. When we live our lives day by day in obedience to the Word of God, then God is glorified in us.

39
Blessed Be The Lord God Almighty

I Completely Forgot My Song

Blessed be the God and Father of our Lord Jesus Christ,
who has blessed us with every spiritual blessing in the heavenly
places in Christ.

—EPHESIANS 1:3

The calling on Bob Fitts's life is to bring hope and encouragement to the people of the world. This vision has been formulated since his senior year in high school, when he had an encounter with Christ that changed his direction completely. He became totally dedicated to the service of his Lord. This was evidenced in the worship and teaching ministry that he started with a friend in high school that resulted in up to one hundred students gathering to participate each week.

During Bob's early childhood years, his father was a Southern Baptist minister in Cleburne, Texas. Bob's dad loved southern gospel music, and that was the music young Bob was exposed to as a child. In his teen years, after his parents moved the family to California,

Bob was greatly influenced by a contemporary Christian music group called the 2nd Chapter of Acts.

Bob received a bachelor's degree in Christian ministry from the Melodyland School of Theology in Anaheim, California. During his college years he also served as Youth Minister at Trinity Christian Center in Riverside, California, and married his college sweetheart, Kathy. In 1982, Bob, Kathy, and eighteen-month-old Andy moved to Hawaii, where they became involved with Youth with a Mission (YWAM). During their twenty years in that island state, God has given them three other children.

It was during the first few months after the Fitts family moved to Hawaii that Bob wrote his very popular song, "Blessed Be the Lord God Almighty." Although he was under the umbrella of YWAM and had agreed to teach in their Discipleship Training School, Bob's initial reason for coming to Hawaii was to write Christian songs. After a short time he found himself becoming involved in so many other activities that his songwriting was being pushed further and further into the background.

Bob became somewhat disenchanted. The poor living conditions that his family was struggling with were adding to the displeasure. The only housing available to the family was an old, run-down building, now owned by YWAM, that had formerly been a shelter for coffee bean pickers.

One night Bob began to talk to the Lord about their situation. As he took out his guitar, it dawned on him that he was to lead worship at a church the next day. He had committed to provide some special music for the service. Bob was having trouble coming up with something to sing, so he decided to write some music particularly for that service. All of a sudden, "Blessed Be the Lord God Almighty" just came out of his heart, lyrics and melody all at once, with virtually no work involved.

As Bob remembers, "The next morning I went to the church, and as I stood up to present my song, I realized that I had completely forgotten it. I had not written it down, so I just could not remember it." Another song that he had known for some time came into his mind, so he sang that one. That experience left him more than a little frustrated. As he was walking home from the church, his new song all came back to him, so he ran to the house and quickly put "Blessed Be the Lord God Almighty" on audiotape. Two years after his wrote it, Bob did a singing tour in which he included his new song, and it was very well received.

Bob's song is known in Europe as "Father in Heaven," the first three words of the verse. It is now making its way into hymnals, thus giving it an opportunity to become better known and loved. This worship song's lyrics are based in Scripture, including Revelation 4:8, "Holy, holy, holy, Lord God Almighty, Who was, and is, and is to come," and Ephesians 1:3, "Blessed be the God and Father of our Lord Jesus Christ."

The song has been included in many recorded projects. Bob has recorded or has been included in a total of twelve albums and CDs, the latest of which is *I Will Bow to You,* on which will appear five of Bob's songs and two of his son Andy's offerings.

Bob and Kathy continue to make their home in Kailua-Kona, Hawaii, with their children Ryan, Garratt, and Mikella. Andy was married in April of 2000.

REFLECTION:

The wonderful aspect of Bob's song is that it is threefold in its scope, as we recognize the marvelous attributes of God, extend our praise to Him, and express our intention of making His name known in all the earth.

40
The Blood Will Never Lose Its Power

If You're Gonna Play, Play

You were not redeemed with corruptible things, like silver or gold, from your aimless conduct received by tradition from your fathers, but with the precious blood of Christ, as of a lamb without blemish and without spot.

—1 PETER 1:18–19

Andraé's music has had by far the most impact on my family and me, and that impact has probably grown over the years because his music is still the greatest." Those words were spoken by CeCe Winans of the famed Winans family, and people all across the world would agree. One would be hard-pressed to name an individual who has made a greater contribution to praise and worship songs across America than Andraé Crouch.

Andraé and his twin sister, Sandra, were born in Los Angeles, California, into a dedicated Christian home. His dad was a lay preacher, and he saw to it that his family was always active in Christian ministry. While Andraé was growing up, his family attended the Emmanuel Church of God in Christ, pastored by Andraé's great-uncle, with a congregation of approximately two thousand people.

Andraé's parents had two dry-cleaning establishments; his dad managed one and his mom the other. They boldly shared their faith whenever the opportunity arose with those who frequented their businesses. "We were always aware of the blessings of the Lord," Andraé shares, "and we wanted to win souls for Him."

One day the call came to Andraé's father to preach at Macedonia Church, a small congregation about sixty miles from Los Angeles. Andraé had never heard his dad preach in a church—on street corners, in hospitals, and in other places, but not in a real pulpit in a church. So that Sunday morning, Andraé and his brother and sister loaded into the car with their parents and headed off to hear Andraé's dad preach.

The congregation at that little church begged Andraé's dad to preach on an interim basis until they could secure a pastor. He was hesitant to do so, so he began to bargain with the Lord. "If You will give Andraé the gift of playing the piano," he prayed, "I will be a full-time minister and figure out some other way to provide for my family." Andraé was dyslexic and stuttered very badly, so his dad knew that he wouldn't be a speaker, but he had hoped that maybe music was in his young son somewhere.

During that first service Andraé's dad called him up from the audience and asked, "Andraé, if God gave you music, would you use it for His glory in your life?" Andraé was only eleven years old and had never thought about it. There were no musicians in his immediate or extended family. He later recalled, "I wouldn't have been more shocked if he had asked, 'Would you like to be an astronaut?'" But Andraé's mother believed so strongly in her husband's prayers that she went to a music store and bought a cardboard piano keyboard for Andraé to practice fingering on. He immediately began to bang on the keyboard, pretending to play music that he had heard on the radio.

During a church service three weeks later, as they were about to sing "What a Friend We Have in Jesus," Andraé's dad called out to him, "Andraé, come up here." He motioned to an upright piano nearby and said, "If you're gonna play, play." He even took the time to show his young son the soft pedal and the expression pedal. ("I haven't to this day figured out what the middle pedal is for," Andraé admits.) When the congregation began to sing, Andraé found the right key and began to play with both hands! About two weeks later his father gave up his dry-cleaning business, and that was the beginning of the ministry of their entire family.

When Andraé was fourteen, he was invited to a friend's home for the church choir's Memorial Day party. When he arrived, people were in the backyard barbecuing and generally having a good time. Andraé was so shy that he didn't want to go out there. Also, he had seen some of the choir members acting in ways that were not Christlike, and he became so disappointed that he began to weep.

Andraé recalls, "I said to the Lord, 'God, I really love You. How can this be? I would love to write songs for You. If you would give me a song, I will live for You forever.' There was a large piano in the living room, and I began to play. The group in the backyard couldn't hear me. I then glanced toward the crowd and saw something that made time, it seemed, go into slow motion. I watched as they slowly poured red sauce onto the meat they were cooking. I couldn't hear for a few moments.

"Suddenly, in my mind's eye I could see Jesus carrying his cross up to Calvary, and I saw His blood. I saw people following Him up the hill where He was to be crucified. As I saw this scene that had been prompted by the activities in the back yard, I said, 'Oh, the blood!' I then turned to my friend Billy Preston, also a pianist, and said, 'Play these chords.' And I began to sing, 'The blood that Jesus shed for me . . .' The people in the backyard heard me singing and came into the house. They began to weep as they came and joined in my song. We sang for about an hour and a half. That was the writing of my first song, 'The Blood Will Never Lose Its Power.'"

Since that day, Andraé Crouch has stood true to the Word of God and continues to share with the world the wonderful music that God has given to him, including "My Tribute" and "Through It All." His well-deserved accolades and accomplishments are far too many to list here.

Rev. Crouch is now the pastor of New Christ Memorial Church in Los Angeles and, along with his sister Sandra, continues to sing for the glory of the Lord, in addition to his preaching.

REFLECTION:

The horror of crucifixion was carried out for nearly one thousand years, with multiplied thousands falling victim to this method of execution. But the only One who died in this manner and then rose again to redeem you and me is our Lord and Savior, Jesus Christ. Truly, His blood will never lose the power to take away our sins.

41
This Is the Day

The Bible as a Songbook

This is the day the LORD has made;
we will rejoice and be glad in it.

—PSALM 118:24

Often during a service the only hymnbook we would have was the Bible. So we sang out of the Bible. I know approximately three hundred songs that we could sing right out of the King James Version of God's Word. Most of the writers of the Scripture songs used the Authorized Version because it is so poetic and easy to put to music. This was part of a great outpouring of Scripture songs in the 1960s." Those are the memories of Les Garrett, who lives in Australia and is the author of one of the most popular Christian songs in the world today.

Les was born in Matamata, New Zealand, and had nothing in his early childhood, his teen years, or even his early adult life to suggest that he would write a song of any sort, not to mention a song of great popularity. His love for God and his thirst for the

Bible were the greatest contributing factors in the birth of his song. Les fondly remembers the events that led up to the writing of "This Is the Day."

When Les was twenty-four, he and his family moved to Australia and were living in Brisbane, Queensland. The Garretts were going through a difficult time in their lives. Les was ministering as a traveling evangelist and was going through a bit of a valley. They had very little money and couldn't even afford gas for their car.

Les was reading his Bible through on his knees, and on this particular day he was reading in Psalm 118. When he came to verse 24, he paused and read the verse a second time, and as he did a tune suddenly came to him. He simply was reading his Bible and worshiping the Lord, with no thought of writing a song. Les admits, "I have very little musical ability and do not play an instrument; therefore, I can only believe that it was a gift from God."

He didn't teach the song to anyone for two years. The more he sang it, the more he thought, *Well, it is just a little thing that God has given to bless me with.*

Near the end of 1969, Les was asked to return to New Zealand to speak at a camp being held in a tent pitched by a river. One night during a meeting, the pastor of the church sponsoring the camp said, "Does anyone have anything that he or she would like to share before Pastor Garrett speaks?" An elderly lady stood, looked straight at Les, and said, "There is someone here who has something that was given to you by the Lord, and you are not sharing it. God has given you something that you are supposed to share."

As she sat down Les felt real conviction that he had never shared his song. So he stood up and said, "I think that message is for me. I have a song that the Lord gave to me, and I have been singing it for a couple of years. I want to teach it to you tonight."

The lyrics of the song are directly from Psalm 118:24: "This is the day the LORD has made; we will rejoice and be glad in it." The repeated phrases of the song, sung to Les's lilting tune, make it a happy song indeed, enjoyed by worshipers of all age groups. Christian Copyright Licensing International consistently reports it in their Top 25 list of worship songs.

From that camp, "This Is the Day" was spread over New Zealand to the extent that in six months it was being sung throughout the whole island nation. The following year it was published in the first edition of the famed *Scripture in Song* series of songbooks, published in Australia by David Garratt. That publication launched "This Is the Day" on its journey around the world. Les has heard his song sung in many of the twenty-three nations where he has preached.

Les didn't copyright the song for ten years. He thought, *It is the Lord's song, so why should I copyright it?* He knew that it was from the Lord for the church. However, in 1987, Les was persuaded by a guest pastor from the United States to copyright the song, and the royalties from the publishers have helped to finance his preaching trips abroad. In addition to other countries, he travels and speaks twice each year in the United States.

Many people will be astonished to learn that "This Is the Day" is the only song Les has ever written. He admits, "I did get a quickening about another verse in the Psalms years ago, but I didn't write it down, so it left me."

Les pastored churches for twenty-eight years in the cities of New Plymouth and Perth in Australia, but for the past five to six years has had a full-time traveling ministry. Grandfather Les Garrett—with three grown children and three grandchildren—now resides with his wife, Caroline, in Queensland on the east coast of Australia.

REFLECTION:

"This Is the Day" is a Scripture song that is easy to sing but difficult to live by. Let us fix our eyes on the victory that can be ours if we can rejoice and be glad to know that each day belongs to the Lord.

42
Oh the Glory of Your Presence

The Inspiration of Solomon's Prayer

You will show me the path of life; in Your presence is fullness of joy;
at Your right hand are pleasures forevermore.

—PSALM 16:11

By age four, Steve Fry began singing to crowds of up to two thousand people in his dad's revival services. Those were only small indications of things to come. Steve's love for music grew so intense that by the time he was in the ninth grade he had written a full piano concerto. He credits his piano teacher, Carol Griffin, for encouraging his musical creativity.

Steven Fry was born in Orange County, California, into the home of Assembly of God pastors Gerry and Peggy Fry. He started his formal music training in elementary school. In the young adult phase of his ministry he had the privilege of working with his parents in a large church that experienced the presence and the blessings of God.

Steve is quick to recognize that his music, as well as his life, has been impacted with the classic hymns of the church—hymns such as "Praise to the Lord, the Almighty" and "All Creatures of Our God and King." Steve's philosophy of worship is that Christians should have an active role in praising and glorifying God, as opposed to merely observing the worship of others who happen to be on the platform. As he says, "Worship allows truth in the mind to seep deep into the heart."

In order to comprehend the story behind Steve's popular worship song "Oh the Glory of Your Presence," one needs to understand a little of the spiritual environment that birthed it. When Steve's dad became the pastor of Calvary Community Church, a small congregation of 125 people in the San Jose, California, area, he was told that it was a pastor's graveyard. But Steve's dad had been completely captivated by two precepts: the glory of the Lord and the concept of worship as the church's most important ministry.

With those two overriding guidelines in place, the church grew to four thousand in attendance in a matter of a few years. It was built on the presence of God, and not on a program. Steve was profoundly affected by the philosophy of his dad, who said, "Success doesn't matter anymore. I want the presence of God, no matter how large or small the church, no matter how wide or how limited my ministry may be."

Steve became the youth pastor of the church, and with a great emphasis on worship, he saw a handful of kids grow to a group of more than seven hundred. From his youth group, Steve was able to build a teen choir of 120 voices that had a marvelous opportunity to minister.

At age twenty-three, while still the youth pastor, Steve was in his parents' living room sitting at the small spinet piano worshiping the Lord. He recalls, "I had an overwhelming sense that the glory of God is all we need as Christians. With His presence comes the fullness of everything else. In Psalm 16:11, God says, 'You will show me the path of life; in Your presence is fullness of joy; at Your right hand are pleasures forevermore.' I was overcome by that truth and began to write, 'Oh the glory of Your presence . . .'"

The lyrics of Steve's song are thought-provoking indeed. He not only recognizes Christians as "temples" of God, but he goes back to Solomon's prayer in 2 Chronicles 6 for another line of the song: "So arise to Your rest and be blessed by our praise." In Steve's song, as in Solomon's prayer, we rejoice and glory in the embrace of our God as His presence fills our very lives. On the wings of the beautiful melody that the Lord gave to Steve, this worship song has made its way around the world.

Steve and his wife, Nancy, now reside in the Nashville area with their three children, Cameron, Kelsey, and Caleigh. Steve continues his busy schedule of travel as well as his writing. To date he has written some 250 songs and several very popular musicals, one of which was nominated for a Dove Award.

REFLECTION:

When we go from the presence of God into the world, we will see those around us as souls with an eternal destiny. We will become acutely aware that each of them is a person for whom Christ died, in order to also bring them into His presence.

43
He Is Exalted

Beyond the People Who Know My Name

The LORD is exalted, for He dwells on high.

—ISAIAH 33:5

My songs are like children who will grow and expand and do things I could never do. They make their way around the world as they are being used for the purpose that God gave them. A song that was given to me in a time of worship is now offered back to Him on a Sunday morning in a small church on a faraway island. 'He Is Exalted' has gone far beyond the people who know my name." Those are comments of Twila Paris as she explains her reasons for continuing to write worship songs. Twila is one of today's most prominent songwriters of praise and worship music.

Twila, a preacher's kid, was born in Fort Worth, Texas. She grew up with music all around her, starting her singing experience at the age of two in her dad's services. Like many preachers' kids, Twila came to know the Lord at a young age. As she grew older, her dad, a pianist of extraordinary talent, began to teach her music and to challenge her creativity. She wrote her first recorded song at age seventeen.

When Twila was eighteen, she faced a crossroads in her spiritual walk and made a crucial decision: "I determined that I would submit my ambitions and the goals that I had set for my life to the Lord. I laid them at His feet and became willing to embark on what He called me to do."

After finishing high school, Twila enrolled for one year in the discipleship program of Youth with a Mission, thinking that she would enter college the following year. One year of ministry turned into two, and by then she was already writing and recording songs, so she continued in her music ministry.

Twila wrote the song "He Is Exalted" in the living room of her parents' home. The Paris family had a used studio piano in the room, which was the center of the house. Twila vividly remembers the experience. "As was my custom, I was sitting at the piano worshiping the Lord for a period of time. I would usually start singing—one of my songs or a song written by someone else that happened to be meaningful at that particular point in my life. As I was there before Him, 'He Is Exalted' was given to me by my heavenly Father. I recognized the moment and knew that this gift from the Lord was something extra-special. It was like taking dictation."

Twila first sang "He Is Exalted" in a Sunday service at the Youth with a Mission base in Arkansas, where she served as a worship leader. After the song had been used in numerous worship services, Twila included it on her *Kingdom Seekers* album, recorded in 1985. Several years later she became aware that many people in churches across the country seemed to know her song.

One day Twila was watching a television news show, and the story being reported was of a religious nature. During the newscaster's comments, the station cut away to a congregation singing "He Is Exalted." Recalls Twila, "For several moments it was almost surreal. It took me a few seconds to realize, 'Hey, that's my song.'" She then added, "I hope I never get used to hearing my songs."

After a friend brought the news from Brazil that the people in that country were singing "He Is Exalted" in Portuguese, Twila was so thrilled about it she asked if she might obtain a copy of the song in Portuguese. She then memorized the song and sang it on her album *Sanctuary*.

In the twenty years that Twila has been writing, the Lord has given her approximately two hundred songs, most of which have been recorded or published. When she considers the ministry of songwriting the Lord has graciously given, she thinks of the impact the songs have had on the world—and she is grateful.

Twila and her husband, Jack Wright, reside in Elm Springs, Arkansas, and continue their involvement with Youth with a Mission. On April 29, 2001, after sixteen years of marriage and many sincere prayers, God blessed their lives with their first child, Jack Paris Wright.

REFLECTION:

One of Twila's favorite verses of Scripture is Romans 11:36: "For of Him and through Him and to Him are all things, to whom be glory forever." No matter what our heavenly Father gives to us—whether a song, a verse of Scripture, or a word of encouragement—we should gladly share it, through His power, with the body of Christ, and they in turn will offer it back to Him.

44
Here We Are

When Contemporary Wasn't "Cool"

I will praise You, O LORD, with my whole heart;
I will tell of all Your marvelous works.

—PSALM 9:1

Dallas Holm has greatly influenced the world of Christian music with his songs and his singing. He was the first contemporary artist to win Dove Awards for Song of the Year, Songwriter of the Year, and Male Vocalist of the Year. One of his songs, "Rise Again," set music chart records that have not been surpassed for more than a quarter century.

Dallas grew up in St. Paul, Minnesota, in a Christian family, but by age sixteen he was playing in rock bands for dances and parties of which his parents did not approve. So one Sunday evening, his pastor confronted Dallas about his life. Dallas knew that he needed to be changed, and when the pastor confronted him with the claims of the Bible, Dallas made the decision to trust Jesus Christ as his personal Savior. He recalls, "When I became a Christian, along with the

178

commitment of my life to the Lord was a commitment of my music—I would only write for Him."

As a young Christian, Dallas was interested in contemporary music. He felt that there must be some way that he could use drums and electric guitars to serve the Lord. At that time the term "contemporary Christian music" had not even been invented, but he remembers going to jails, rest homes, street corners, and small conservative churches in the St. Paul area to present the "praise" music of his small band. On more than one occasion their engagements were cut short in churches by pastors who would graciously explain why Dallas couldn't or shouldn't do that kind of music in church. To borrow an expression from our country music friends, Dallas "was contemporary when contemporary wasn't cool."

In 1970, evangelist David Wilkerson, author of *The Cross and the Switchblade,* asked Dallas to join him in his youth crusade ministry as soloist and song leader. By 1976, Dallas had formed a band, Dallas Holm and Praise, as part of the Wilkerson team.

Dallas considers "Here We Are" the first praise and worship song that he consciously wrote. The inspiration for the song came while Dallas was doing a radio interview in Carlinville, Illinois, in 1974. The disc jockey asked him, "Where did music come from?" Taken by surprise, Dallas first started thinking of his earliest influences in music. Then he thought of classical music, born many years ago. As his mind raced further back, he realized that before the beginning of time there was heavenly music. He finally realized the truth that music comes from God. He told the disc jockey, "Music is an eternal thing. God is the Creator of music."

The disc jockey then asked, "If that is the case, then what should be the primary function and purpose of music?" As Dallas considered his answer, he realized that a lot of his own music was evangelistic or testimonial. But following the disc jockey's line of thought, he answered, "The primary purpose of music is to bring praise, worship, and honor to the Lord. It is something that pleases God." The disc jockey smiled his approval.

Dallas then realized that there was a whole realm of music that he hadn't even thought about. He had only considered the evangelistic slant of his songs, but he began to see that the greater or primary purpose of his music should be to bring glory to God. As he thought on those things, Dallas prayed, "Lord, I want to write something that You want to hear. I want to say words and write songs that please You." He then wrote "Here We Are."

About this experience Dallas says, "That was a big moment in my musical life. It opened a doorway of musical expression for me, which I go through occasionally and write songs just for the Lord, not for people. I have some songs that probably will never show up on a recording. Maybe no one would even like them, but I believe God likes them."

In 1976, "Here We Are" appeared on *Tell 'em Again,* the second album of Dallas Holm and Praise. The song received a lot of radio play and appeared in several publications, in the process making its way around the United States and into other countries.

Dallas summarizes his goal in life as this: "When I stand before the Lord, it won't be how many records I've sold or how many people saw me in concert. What we do for Him is never as important as who we are in Him. That's all He's measuring."

REFLECTION:

There are times when we consciously recognize that we are in the presence of God, but because of His omnipresence we are always and forever where He is. From our rising up in the mornings to our falling asleep at night, we are constantly in His loving care.

45
Think about His Love

Two Blessings at the Tabernacle

Whoever is wise will observe these things, and they
will understand the lovingkindness of the LORD.

—PSALM 107:43

At age nineteen, he sang in the choir of the nationally famous Old Fashioned Revival Hour radio broadcast originating from Long Beach, California. For twenty-four years, he was the director of the Haven singers, formerly known as the Haven of Rest Quartet, who regularly appeared on the syndicated Haven Ministries radio broadcast. He has written five hundred Christian songs, some of which are used in churches worldwide. His musicals are published by Word, and he has recorded albums of songs for Integrity Music and Maranatha! Music. He has been a session singer for the Oscars, Disney Attractions, and the Tonight Show. He wrote the extremely popular worship song "Think about His Love." Such has been the extraordinary career of Christian singer and songwriter Walt Harrah.

Although Walt has lived in California for most of his life, he was born in St. Louis Missouri, as one of eight children in a pastor's family. Walt's parents saw to it that little Walt was singing in church with the family by age four. He played in a school band as early as the fifth grade. As Walt grew older he entered the University of Southern California, where he graduated with a degree in church music and then earned a Master of Divinity degree from Fuller Theological Seminary.

Walt's well-known worship song "Think about His Love" came in a manner that was not necessarily unique to this particular composition. In 1987, as was his custom, Walt was at home enjoying his daily quiet time with the Lord. As a composer he was going through a particularly creative period when he was writing songs quite regularly.

Walt was reading and trying to be obedient to Psalm 107:43: "Whoever is wise will observe these things, and they will understand the lovingkindness of the LORD." After he read this scripture, meditated on it, and prayed, he then wrote down some rough lyrical ideas that suggest that we forget about ourselves and our own circumstances and think instead about God's lovingkindness, mercy, and goodness.

Walt admits, "I don't remember a single song that I have written that came to me instantaneously. So, true to my customs, I took my ideas and then began my usual process of writing and rewriting, tweaking and changing parts of the song here and there. It is a process of refining and improving my work. With this particular project I must have gone through fifteen to twenty rewrites—often coming back to it and looking it over very carefully. The whole process took several days."

The first church service in which "Think about His Love" was used was at Newport Mesa Christian Center in Costa Mesa, California. However, the most meaningful time for Walt to hear his song was on a Sunday morning at the Brooklyn Tabernacle in New York City. Haven, the group in which Walt sang, was invited to minister at that church for the morning and evening services. He says, "As we were ushered into the morning service, the congregation was singing at the top of their lungs, with the most exquisite fervor imaginable. And they were singing 'Think about His Love.' It was overwhelming. It is the greatest privilege to be allowed to write a song and then to see it being used of God in that manner."

Walt and his wife, Sherry, have three children, Mindy, Beth Anne, and Drew. At the time of this writing Walt has just resigned his position with Haven Ministries after twenty-four years. He is now a worship leader at Grace Evangelical Free Church in La Mirada, California, and has been engaged by Biola University to train The Kingsmen, a male vocal ensemble, as musical representatives of the school. Beginning in the fall of 2003, he will assist Biola in a new department designed to teach worship leaders the true essence of worship and praise. He continues to contribute wonderful praise and worship songs to the Christian music world.

REFLECTION:

Our imaginations are not stretched in the slightest when we are asked to "think about His love." Every good, right, and holy thing that we are allowed to experience is a reminder of God's love and goodness.

46
Our God Reigns

From Dark Despair to Total Triumph

How beautiful upon the mountains are the feet of him who brings good news, who proclaims peace, who brings glad tidings of good things, who proclaims salvation, who says to Zion, "Your God reigns!"

—ISAIAH 52:7

Iwas fired from every high school I taught in, public or Catholic. I would have kids finish their assignments in four days and on Fridays I asked them to bring their Bibles. All day long we studied God's Word. I brought my guitar, and we sang songs together. I had a great time, but it was too much for the school authorities to handle. So they all fired me—from four different high schools." That was Leonard Smith's assessment of his teaching career after nine years of college training and five years as a high school teacher.

Leonard, a native of Philadelphia, Pennsylvania, had an early interest in music: a total fascination with the Sons of the Pioneers, a western group that had Roy Rogers as a member early in their career. After all these years, Leonard still remembers their famed rendition of "Cool Water."

His father, a Protestant who never attended church, and his mother, a devout Catholic who attended church regularly, agreed before they married that any children born to them would be raised Protestant. For that reason, Leonard's mother dropped him and his sisters off on Sundays at Blackwood Terrace Community Church.

It was at a Bible class at church that Leonard heard the good news of Jesus and His death on the cross. Leonard believed in Jesus and immediately experienced great happiness. The Sunday school teacher then told Leonard that God was his Father, which was extremely meaningful to him, since at that very time his parents were separating and his earthly father was leaving him. That day Leonard's life was transformed.

In an effort to keep the remainder of the family together, Leonard and his sisters asked if they could attend church with their mother. Leonard became so intrigued with the Catholic Church that he entered college directly after high school and began to study for the priesthood. He received a bachelor's degree in classical philosophy and then studied at Villanova University toward a master's degree in English literature. He also entered Mount St. Mary's Seminary in Emmitsburg, Maryland, and worked toward a master's degree in theology.

As he was continuing to study for the priesthood, one day, quite abruptly, Leonard sensed the Lord saying to him, "It is time to leave, and you are to leave quickly." Leonard quickly obeyed and then began his high school teaching career. He taught in three Catholic high schools and one public high school.

By 1973, for reasons already mentioned, Leonard had rendered himself practically unemployable in the education world, on the high school level. By then, he and his wife, Marian, had two children. Leonard sought employment wherever he could find work, such as painting houses and carpentry. It was difficult to meet former students and try to explain to them what he was doing. Leonard was frustrated because he considered himself a highly educated man being forced to do menial, blue-collar work. His employment situation reduced him to an extremely depressed state.

Leonard came home one day in this grim, dejected condition and sat down to read the Bible. During those days he was reading the Bible two to three hours every day. He had been reading through the Book of Isaiah, and that particular evening his attention was drawn to Isaiah 52:6–7: "Therefore My people shall know My name; therefore they shall know in that day that I am He who speaks: 'Behold, it is I.' How beautiful upon the mountains are the feet of him who brings good news, who proclaims peace, who brings glad tidings of good things, who proclaims salvation, who says to Zion, 'Your God reigns!'"

Leonard remembers, "I immediately thought of Jesus' feet. I realize that most people think of missionaries when they read verse seven, but that never entered my mind. As I read the passage and came to the words "Your God reigns!" it seemed as if the Lord definitely spoke to my heart. His message to me was, 'I know you are out of work, I know you are depressed, and I know you feel like a failure, but these are My doings. I will bring you through this and you will shine as the sun. Everything is fine!'"

Leonard was so comforted he began to weep. And though he had already written about fifty songs and had no thought of writing a song at that time, he picked up his guitar and in about ten minutes wrote the song "Our God Reigns." He credits the Lord for giving him "a total and complete gift from heaven." In the days that followed, the song was so encouraging to Leonard that he would often sing it again and again, sometimes for two hours straight.

Several weeks later he presented the song to his church. As he finished, the pastor literally sprang from his chair and said, "Let's sing that again!" They sang "Our God Reigns" several times.

A little more than a year after its writing, Bob Mumford took "Our God Reigns" to a Shepherd's Conference in Kansas City, Missouri, where he was to speak. He taught it to the multitude of pastors gathered there, who in turn took it back to their churches. It was then published by Dave and Dale Garratt in Australia, in one of their Scripture in Song publications. Shortly thereafter, popular singer Evie Tornquist recorded it, greatly accelerating its flight around the world.

Leonard Smith has now written approximately 170 songs and is one of the worship leaders at The Waters, an independent Protestant church in Sewell, New Jersey. God has given the Smiths five children, and the whole family is associated with The Waters church. Leonard's publishing company, New Jerusalem Music, has recently produced a new CD titled *Deep Calls to Deep,* which contains fifteen selections, including all five verses of "Our God Reigns."

REFLECTION:

Often we as Christians find ourselves enduring tough times, only to find out later that God was preparing us in a special, unusual, and sometimes severe manner for a great task to be performed for His glory.

47
Be Exalted, O God

A Songwriter Plays Hooky

Be exalted, O God, above the heavens;
let Your glory be above all the earth.

—PSALM 57:5

I was in a church in Singapore in 1987 when a missionary approached me who had served in Japan for twenty years. She gave me a copy of 'Be Exalted, O God,' in Japanese, and it was extremely meaningful to me. I have now heard my song in approximately sixteen languages. When the royalty printouts come, I always look first not at how much, but where the song has gone." Such is the humble heart of prolific Christian songwriter Brent Chambers when he considers how he came to write one of the most popular praise and worship songs of this or any other generation.

Brent Chambers was born in the beautiful coastal town of Napier, in Hawke's Bay, in the island nation of New Zealand. His parents saw to it that Brent had voice lessons beginning at age five. A few years later, when the Beatles came along, this "southpaw" was so intent on playing the guitar that he learned to play left-handed with the instrument upside-down. By age eleven, Brent had written his first song, and by age seventeen he was in a small band. The following year he became a Christian at a Youth for Christ meeting.

A couple of years later, after a roller coaster ride, Brent realized that he was not at all including Jesus into his life's activities. He somehow knew that he could not be an effective Christian unless Jesus Christ had his whole life. Consequently, he surrendered everything to Christ and from that time, Brent recalls, "even as a new Christian, songs began to pour out of me."

The day that Brent wrote "Be Exalted, O God," he was actually playing hooky from Auckland University, where he was working on a bachelor's degree in the classics. He had finished three years in the Bible College of New Zealand, and not wanting time to get by him, he quickly entered the university.

During the course of his studies, he got behind in some of his assignments and decided to take a few hours off. During the middle of the afternoon, sitting in his one-bedroom apartment with an ancient tape recorder going and a cockatiel squawking in the background, Brent began reading the Bible. He came across Psalm 57:9–11, and the verses seemed particularly meaningful. Brent thought, *Wow! I'd love to be able to put some music to those words; they really stand out to me.* So he picked up his guitar and began to play a tune that the Lord gave him for that scripture.

Be Exalted, O God

That evening, David and Dale Garratt, founders of the Scripture in Song music publishing company, attended a study group held in Brent's home, and during the course of the evening he sang his song for them. David asked Brent to repeat it several times and then began to press him to change the melody in the second line. Although David is a master at determining what makes a good song, Brent resisted the idea of altering the tune that the Lord had given him. During the following years Scripture in Song published about twenty of Brent's compositions, and "Be Exalted, O God" was the only one that did not undergo some revision or modification.

After hearing Brent's song, David asked him, "Do you think maybe God is speaking to you through these words?" Up until that moment he considered "Be Exalted, O God" as just another song that he had written, but when David said those words, Brent's song became his life's call—his heart's desire. He suddenly wanted to give thanks among the people and to sing praises among the nations, and by the grace of God, "Be Exalted, O God" has helped thousands of Christians accomplish that vision.

Brent and his wife, Raewyn, presently live in Hillsborough, Auckland, New Zealand. They have two sons, Nathan and Jonathon. The Chambers are very active in Encounter Christian Center, where Brent plays in one of the praise bands of the church. He has written approximately two thousand songs, scores of which have been recorded and published.

REFLECTION:

In addition to reading the Scriptures daily, you and I would do well to recite the lyrics of this song. It encompasses our thanksgiving and praise to God, as well as our recognition of His love and faithfulness to His children.

48
I Stand in Awe

Trial and Error, and Some Labor

Let all the earth fear the LORD;
let all the inhabitants of the world stand in awe of Him.

—PSALM 33:8

Though he didn't realize it at the time, the talents developed in the early life of Mark Altrogge were later used and continue to be helpful in his extensive ministry as a senior pastor and song-writer.

Mark was born in Shawnee, Oklahoma, in 1950. As a teenager, he became excited about the Beatles. He wanted to play guitar, get into a band, and be just like them. After six months of guitar lessons, Mark, still in his early teens, formed a small band and taught the other members of the group to play their parts. He could hear the harmony—he played mostly by ear—so he taught the other band members which chords to use. This led to an attempt to make a career of rock-'n'-roll music, which lasted until he became a Christian at age twenty-four during an evangelistic crusade.

About a year later, during a Bible study that was studying genuine repentance, Mark truly realized what it meant to surrender his life to the Lord, and he wholeheartedly turned his life over to Christ. Says Mark, "I soon realized that I would have to give up the rock-'n'-roll band. We were playing in places and using music that I knew was not God-glorifying, so I quit the band and began to follow the Lord."

Mark married his wife, Kristi, in February 1980, and since he had a degree in art, he became an itinerant instructor, traveling to five different elementary schools and teaching art to six hundred students. During that same year Brent Detwiller became pastor of Lord of Life Church in Indiana, Pennsylvania, which had been started from a Full Gospel businessmen's Bible study. Mark was asked to be the worship leader.

Mark wrote his popular worship song "I Stand in Awe" in 1988, while serving as worship leader for Lord of Life Church. He had been studying the attributes of God. He cites several books that were influential in his life at the time, including *The Holiness of God,* by R. C. Sproul, *The Knowledge of the Holy,* by A. W. Tozer, and *The Attributes of God,* by Stephen Charnock. The writings of Charles H. Spurgeon were also very meaningful to Mark during this time.

As Mark describes his experience, "I began to reflect on the beautiful truth that God is infinite in each of His attributes: in His beauty, His holiness, and His wisdom. He is unsearchable! We will never come to an end of learning new things about Him—even throughout eternity."

Mark was playing his guitar as he thought on those things, trying to write a song capturing the thoughts of his heart. The first phrase came quite quickly—acclaiming the beauty of God and the marvel of His being. Then came our response to His beauty, a feeling of awe. Mark had an idea for the chorus, but it took him quite a time to work out the completion of the song—several days.

Mark admits that in all of his songwriting, he has had only one song come completely at one sitting. He shares, "For me, writing a song is much like preparing a sermon. I do a lot of writing and rewriting. There is some trial and error. It took a good amount of labor to get 'I Stand in Awe' to a state of completion. I am grateful for the assistance of two friends, Bob Cauflin and Steve Cook, who made suggestions, strengthening the song. At the recommendation of David Clydesdale, I later wrote the second verse, to be used in a musical he was writing."

Mark now pastors the church where he first sang "I Stand in Awe," and from there it has made its way around the world, becoming one of the most requested songs in churches of the United States. He has written more than four hundred songs, with some 150 of them recorded or published. He continues to write songs, along with his duties as senior pastor of Lord of Life Church in Indiana, Pennsylvania.

Mark and Kristi have three sons, Stephen, David, and Jonathan, and one daughter, Beth.

REFLECTION:
Mark's song brings to our minds the realization of the beauty and the majesty of our heavenly Father, which we will only be able to fully realize when we stand before Him in our heavenly home. Then we will know God even as we are known.

49
There Is None Like You

A Notable Crossover

O Lord, there is none like You,
nor is there any God besides You.

—1 Chronicles 17:20

I became involved in music quite by accident. One day I was visiting in a friend's home, and several of the young people there were playing instruments. They asked me if I would sing with them. I agreed to do so, and after a few songs they said, 'You sound pretty good.' I responded, 'I do?' They then asked if I would sing with them in a talent show to be held at the school. I was surprised with their invitation but agreed to participate. While we were singing in the contest, I was so timid I turned my back toward the audience. But we won nonetheless.

"They then asked me to get a bass guitar. I asked, 'What's a bass guitar?' They said, 'It's the one with the four big strings on it.' I said, 'Okay.' So I went to work at Eckerd's to earn enough money to buy a bass guitar and taught myself to play it. I then began to play in small bands, and by the time I was seventeen years of age I was supporting myself with my music." Thus began the musical career of Lenny LeBlanc.

Lenny was born in Leominster, Massachusetts, in 1951. As a young lad, about ten years of age, he became interested in music, but his parents were not financially able to furnish him with any kind of instrument. For this reason his interest in music lay dormant until he was about fifteen. It was during that year that he made the notable visit to his friend's house.

Lenny went on to a very successful career in pop music, at first as a studio musician on recordings for singers such as Crystal Gayle, Joan Baez, Roy Orbison, Hank Williams, Jr., and The Supremes. He then became a part of a duo, LeBlanc and Carr. To the present day, their smash hit, "Falling," a dreamy, romantic ballad cowritten by LeBlanc, remains in the record books as one of the most popular singles ever—remaining on the charts for twenty-seven weeks during 1978 and 1979. It was named a Broadcast Music Incorporated millionaire song, indicating one million radio plays, and was named one of *Billboard's* all-time favorite Top 40 hits.

LeBlanc confessed, "My career was my god and I began to worship the gift God had given me, even to the point of leaving my family behind." Lenny was not at a low point in life, nor was he looking or searching for God when a good friend, an ex-drug smuggler, called him late one night and said, 'Lenny, I got saved and I'm going to heaven.' He then told Lenny, 'I want you to be there with me. Are you saved?' Without thinking Lenny answered, 'Yes,' not even knowing what being saved meant, despite having had some contact with Christian musicians while singing for an Amy Grant project, *My Father's Eyes,* two years earlier.

Lenny's friend sent him a Bible, and for the next few weeks God began to reveal His love to Lenny. He began to realize how shallow and selfish his life was, and he cried out to Jesus for mercy and forgiveness. Lenny could have continued in the field of pop music, but he sensed that God had something different for him.

Musically and financially, Lenny languished in an unpleasant wilderness for two years since he was not able to be released from his contract to Capitol records. Finally, after two years, he gained freedom from the contract and released his first Christian album, *Say a Prayer,* which was warmly received. Thus began a notable crossover, from pop songs into the Lord's music that ministers to so many hearts.

Lenny has had eight solo releases, with more than a dozen Top 10 radio singles. His involvement with Maranatha! Music and Integrity Incorporated has brought him before large Christian audiences. As a songwriter Lenny primarily writes Christian songs, but he occasionally pens solid relational songs like the number one country hit "Treat Her Right" for Sawyer Brown and "Father Knows Best" for Ricky Skaggs.

In 1991, Lenny was asked by Integrity Music to be the worship leader on the CD project *Pure Heart,* so he tried to carve out time from his schedule to write some songs for the endeavor. One morning, while at home alone, he was playing the keyboard when suddenly a tune and some lyrics began coming to him. Before long, he had written the major part of a song, which he titled "There Is None Like You." Lenny was so overwhelmed by the Spirit of God that he began to weep. He found it hard to believe that God would give him such a wonderful song. Because it was so meaningful to him, Lenny soon had it committed to memory.

A few weeks later Lenny participated in a "song meeting," in Mobile, Alabama, concerning the selections for the album *Pure Heart.* When Lenny played the song for the group, they immediately expressed their appreciation for it and seemed to agree unanimously that it would be a good song for the project.

Orchestra tracks were prerecorded in preparation for the live recording. They chose Faith Tabernacle in Florence, Alabama, as the location for the session. The choir and Lenny were the only ones on the platform. Lenny and Kelly Willard performed "There Is None Like You" as a duet; her part was on tape, while Lenny sang his part live. *Pure Heart* launched "There Is None Like You" on its way into the hearts of Christians and churches around the world.

Three years ago Lenny accompanied Don Moen to Korea, where they were engaged in some extraordinary meetings in an outdoor square with sixty thousand young people. During one of the sessions they sang "There Is None Like You." Don then asked them to sing it in their own language. Much to Lenny's surprise, they already knew it. Lenny was not aware of it, but the song had been translated into Korean some time before. Someone there asked him, "Didn't you know that your song is one of the most popular Christian songs, if not the most popular, throughout all of Asia?" He was completely overwhelmed. To date, the song has been translated into at least a half-dozen languages in the Orient.

Lenny and his wife, Sherrie, have for a number of years lived in Muscle Shoals, a small town in northern Alabama. They have two daughters, Hannah and Noelle. Lenny is the proprietor of a recording studio in that city and continues to travel, singing in scores of concerts each year. He is worship leader and coordinates the total music ministry for Faith Tabernacle in Florence. He also continues to write, with up to four hundred songs completed and more than 150 of those already recorded or published.

REFLECTION:
As we read through the Scriptures and consider all of our Lord's wonderful deeds, His lovingkindness, and the works of His hands, we realize, like Lenny's song proclaims, that truly there is no one like our wonderful God.

50
Come into His Presence

From the Hiking Trail to the Filing Cabinet

Let us come before His presence with thanksgiving;
let us shout joyfully to Him with psalms.

—PSALM 95:2

I had never submitted a song to Integrity, or to any other publisher, and yet they had recorded my song on one of their cassette projects. It was listed in the credits as 'author unknown.' Two days after I heard the tape for the first time I called Integrity and said, 'I am "author unknown," the writer of one of the songs on your latest tape project.' They made no hesitation in recognizing me as the writer and told me, 'We have been setting royalties aside hoping we could find you.'" This story, told by Christian songwriter Lynn Baird, is only a part of a most interesting story behind one of the most famous praise songs of all time.

Lynn was born in 1952 in Phoenix, Arizona. His mother was a musician of sorts and could play the piano in a limited fashion. His dad, according to Lynn, "had little trouble carrying a tune—he just couldn't unload it." Nevertheless, they were both very supportive of Lynn.

Lynn came to know the Lord at the age of six, after discussing his need for salvation with the pastor. Along with his three brothers and one sister, Lynn was active in the graded choir program of First Southern Baptist Church in Glendale, Arizona. As a senior in high school he started a band called Unity. The band continued to play together through Lynn's college years at Grand Canyon University, where he graduated with a degree in music. He then taught vocal music for two years at Washington High School in Glendale.

In the early 1970s, while still playing in the band Unity, Lynn started a coffeehouse for young people to come, have refreshments, and hear Christian music along with a message from the Bible. It grew to the extent that a couple hundred people attended each weekend.

The band members of Unity started a very successful Bible study with those who frequented the coffeehouse. Out of this group grew a new church called Foundation Fellowship. Lynn became one of the pastors and was in charge of the music ministry. He often wrote songs for their worship on Sunday mornings. This gave him tremendous encouragement, plus an outlet for his songwriting.

In the mid 1970s, Lynn's family went to a place called Oak Creek in northern Arizona, a place where they had vacationed for years. They were staying in a mobile home in that resort area, surrounded by riverbeds and streams. During the vacation, Lynn decided to go for a hike one day. While he was walking through those wilderness places, the Lord dropped a melody and some lyrics into his mind. As soon as he was able to do so he found something— he doesn't remember what—and wrote it all down. When he got to an instrument where he could play and sing the song, he became skeptical that it would even work, so he simply filed it away.

One day, perhaps a year later, Lynn was sitting in his office when a good friend, who was a musician in their church and a cellist in a local orchestra, came by. Lynn said, "Let me play a song for you to see what you think." He pulled his song out of the files and played it for him. Lynn's friend was favorably impressed and suggested that they use the song in their services. They then presented it to the praise band, who prepared to sing it during a Sunday morning service. It was so well received that they sang it in subsequent services. The congregation continued to sing it for five to six years—until it became old to them.

In 1986, about ten years after writing "Come into His Presence," Lynn planted a new church in Tempe, Arizona, and he became the senior pastor. About a year later he attended a leadership retreat at Camel Back Inn in Scottsdale, Arizona. Before the first morning session began, a gentleman who was to be the worship leader for the retreat mentioned that Integrity had come out with a new praise and worship tape. Lynn and his fellow musicians all anxiously awaited new tapes from Integrity to get more worship materials. The gentleman offered to play the tape for Lynn. When he did so, Lynn was astounded to hear that the first song was "Come into His Presence." He excitedly announced, "That is my song! I wonder how they got it!" To add to his surprise, on the tape case, among the credits, the song was listed as "author unknown." To this day it has never been determined how Integrity got Lynn's song.

"Come into His Presence" has circled the globe and has extended the ministry of Lynn Baird a thousandfold. And though he continues to write songs for Abundant Life Community Church in Pasadena, California, where he is a pastor, "Come into His Presence," as of this writing, is his only published song out of his more than one hundred praise choruses and worship songs. And yet there seems to be no ceiling to the heights to which this song will go. It is found in hymnals, in children's projects, on exercise tapes, on the *Songs 4 Worship* CD series, and in chorus books, just to name a few places.

Lynn and his wife, Terri, have three sons and one daughter. They make their home in Pasadena, California.

REFLECTION:

Lynn's song reminds us of two Scripture passages, one of which is Psalm 100. In that favorite psalm, God lets us know that when we come into His presence, He is pleased to have us praise Him, sing to Him, and be thankful to Him.

Sources / Song Acknowledgments

Sources

Bill and Gloria Gaither—Because He Lives

Gloria Gaither, *Fully Alive* (Alexandria, Ind.: Gaither Music Company, 1984). Used by permission of Gloria Gaither.

Jack Hayford—Majesty

Dr. Jack Hayford, *Worship His Majesty* (Dallas: Word, 1987). Used by permission of Dr. Hayford.

Graham Kendrick—Shine, Jesus, Shine

The Official Graham Kendrick Web site, www.grahamkendrick.co.uk. Used by permission.

Rich Mullins—I Pledge Allegiance to the Lamb

Melissa Riddle, "Rich Hope for the Church," *Worship Leader,* November/December 1997. Used by permission of Chuck Fromm, Executive Editor.

Song Acknowledgments

Akers, Doris. "Sweet, Sweet, Spirit." Copyright © 1962, renewed 1990 by Manna Music, Inc.

Altrogge, Mark. "I Stand in Awe." Copyright © 1988 PDI Praise. BMI.

Crouch, Andraé. "The Blood Will Never Lose Its Power." Copyright © 1966, renewed 1994 by Manna Music, Inc.

Baird, Lynn. "Come into His Presence." Copyright © 1988 Integrity's Hosanna! Music. c/o Integrity Music, Inc.

Sources / Song Acknowledgments

Baloche, Paul. "Open the Eyes of My Heart." Copyright © 1997 Integrity's Hosanna! Music c/o Integrity Music, Inc. ASCAP.

Boltz, Ray. "I Pledge Allegiance to the Lamb." Copyright © 1994 Word Music (a division of Word, Inc.) / Shepherd Boy Music.

Chambers, Brent. "Be Exalted, O God." Copyright © 1977 Scripture in Song (a division of Integrity Music, Inc.).

Davis, Geron. "Holy Ground." Copyright © 1983 Meadowgreen Music. ASCAP.

Dearman, Kirk and Deby. "We Bring the Sacrifice of Praise." Copyright © 1984 John T. Benson Publishing Co., Inc. ASCAP.

DeShazo, Lynn. "More Precious Than Silver." Copyright © 1982 Integrity's Hosanna! Music c/o Integrity Music, Inc. ASCAP.

Espinosa, Eddie. "Change My Heart, O God." Copyright © 1982 Mercy / Vineyard Publishing. ASCAP.

Fitts, Bob. "Blessed Be the Lord God Almighty." Copyright © 1984 Scripture in Song (a division of Integrity Music, Inc.). ASCAP.

Founds, Rick. "Lord, I Lift Your Name on High." Copyright © 1989 Maranatha Praise, Inc. (administered by The Copyright Company, Nashville, Tenn.). ASCAP.

Fry, Steve. "Oh the Glory of Your Presence." Copyright © 1983 BMG Songs, Inc. / Birdwing Music. ASCAP.

Gaither, Gloria and William J. "Because He Lives." Copyright © 1971, 1979 William J. Gaither.

Gardner, Daniel. "My Life Is in You, Lord." Copyright © 1986 Integrity's Hosanna! Music c/o Integrity Music, Inc. ASCAP.

Garrett, Les. "This Is the Day." Copyright © 1990 Integrity's Hosanna! Music c/o Integrity Music, Inc. ASCAP.

Sources/Song Acknowledgments

Goss, Roni. "I Want to Do Thy Will, O Lord." Copyright © 1965 Silverline Music, Inc., Nashville, Tenn.

Harrah, Walt. "Think about His Love." Copyright © 1987 Integrity's Hosanna! Music c/o Integrity Music, Inc.

Hayford, Jack. "Majesty." Copyright © 1981 Rocksmith Music (administered by Trust Music Management). ASCAP.

Hearn, Naida. "Jesus, Name Above All Names." Copyright © 1974 Scripture in Song (a division of Integrity Music, Inc.). ASCAP.

Holm, Dallas. "Here We Are." Copyright © 1978 Dimension Music / SESAC (all rights controlled by The Benson Company, Inc.).

Jernigan, Dennis. "You Are My All in All." Copyright © 1991 Shepherd's Heart Music, Inc. (administered by Dayspring Music, Inc.). CMI.

Kaiser, Kurt. "Oh How He Loves You and Me." Copyright © 1975 Word Music, Inc. ASCAP.

Kendrick, Graham. "Shine, Jesus, Shine." Copyright © 1987 Make Way Music (administered by Music Services in the Western Hemisphere). ASCAP.

Kilpatrick, Bob. "Lord, Be Glorified." Copyright © 1978 Bob Kilpatrick. ASCAP.

Klein, Laurie. "I Love You, Lord." Copyright © 1978 House of Mercy Music c/o Maranatha! Music (administered by The Copyright Company, Nashville, Tenn.). ASCAP.

Lafferty, Karen. "Seek Ye First." Copyright © 1972 Maranatha! Music (administered by The Copyright Company, Nashville, Tenn.). ASCAP.

LeBlanc, Lenny. "There Is None Like You." Copyright © 1991 Integrity's Hosanna! Music c/o Integrity Music, Inc. ASCAP.

Sources / Song Acknowledgments

MacAlmon, Terry. "I Sing Praises." Copyright © 1989 Integrity's Hosanna! Music c/o Integrity Music, Inc. ASCAP.

McGuire, Dony and Reba. "A Perfect Heart." Copyright © 1980 Bud John Songs, Inc. / Ooh's and Ah's Music / Makanume Music.

Mieir, Audrey. "His Name Is Wonderful." Copyright © 1958, renewed 1987 Manna Music, Inc. ASCAP.

Moen, Don. "God Will Make a Way." Copyright © 1990 Integrity's Hosanna! Music c/o Integrity Music, Inc. ASCAP.

Moen, Don. "I Want to Be Where You Are." Copyright © 1989 Integrity's Hosanna! Music c/o Integrity Music, Inc. ASCAP.

Moody, David. "All Hail, King Jesus." Copyright © 1980 Dayspring Music, Inc. BMI.

Mullins, Rich. "Awesome God." Copyright © 1988 BMG Songs, Inc. ASCAP.

Nelson, Greg and Phill McHugh. "People Need the Lord." Copyright © 1983 River Oaks Music Company (a division of the Sparrow Corporation) / Shepherd's Fold Music (a division of Star Song Communications, Inc.) (administered by Gaither Copyright Management).

Newton, John. "Amazing Grace." Public domain.

Nystrom, Marty. "As the Deer." Copyright © 1984 Maranatha Praise, Inc. (administered by The Copyright Company, Nashville, Tenn.). ASCAP.

Oliver, Gary. "Celebrate Jesus." Copyright © 1967 Scripture in Song (a division of Integrity Music, Inc.). ASCAP.

Paris, Twila. "He Is Exalted." Copyright © 1985 Straightway Music / Mountain Spring Music. ASCAP.

Perronet, Edward. "All Hail the Power of Jesus' Name." Public domain.

Sources/Song Acknowledgments

Rambo, Dottie. "I Will Glory in the Cross." Copyright © 1978 John T. Benson Company. ASCAP.

Rambo, Dottie. "We Shall Behold Him." Copyright © 1980 John T. Benson Company.

Sanchez, Jr., Pete. "I Exalt Thee." Copyright © 1977 Gabriel Music. ASCAP.

Scriven, Joseph. "What a Friend We Have in Jesus." Public domain.

Smith, Henry. "Give Thanks." Copyright ©1978 Integrity's Hosanna! Music c/o Integrity Music, Inc. ASCAP.

Smith, Leonard. "Our God Reigns." Copyright © 1974, 1978 Leonard Smith, Jr., New Jerusalem Music.

Smith, Michael W. and Deborah. "Great Is the Lord." Copyright © 1982 Meadowgreen Music Company (administered by EMI Christian Music Publishing). ASCAP.

Tunney, Dick and Melodie and Paul Smith. "How Excellent Is Thy Name." Copyright © 1985 BMG Songs, Inc. / Pamela Kay Music / Marquis III Music / Word Music, Inc. ASCAP.

Von Brethorst, Leona. "He Has Made Me Glad." Copyright © 1976 Maranatha Praise, Inc. (administered by The Copyright Company, Nashville, Tenn.). ASCAP.

Wolfe, Lanny. "More Than Wonderful." Copyright © 1982 Lanny Wolfe Music (all rights controlled by Pathway Music, Cleveland, Tenn.). ASCAP.

Wolfe, Lanny. "Surely the Presence of the Lord." Copyright © 1977 Lanny Wolfe Company. ASCAP.

Wood, Sondra Corbett. "I Worship You, Almighty God." Copyright © 1983 Integrity's Hosanna! Music c/o Integrity Music, Inc. ASCAP.

Sources / Song Acknowledgments

Zschech, Darlene. "Shout to the Lord." Copyright © 1993 Darlene Zschech /
Hillsongs, Australia (administered in the U.S. and Canada by Integrity's
Hosanna! Music c/o Integrity Music, Inc.). ASCAP.

Index of Songs

Index

Index